The Great Plains Guide to
BUFFALO BILL

*To Grant —
With my best!*

4/10/2014

The Great Plains Guide to
BUFFALO BILL

FORTS, FIGHTS
& OTHER SITES

Jeff Barnes

STACKPOLE
BOOKS

To Carter Scott

Published by
STACKPOLE BOOKS
5067 Ritter Road
Mechanicsburg, PA 17055
www.stackpolebooks.com

Printed in the United States of America

10 9 8 7 6 5 4 3 2 1

FIRST EDITION

Cover design by Caroline M. Stover
All interior photos by the author or from the author's collection unless noted

Library of Congress Cataloging-in-Publication Data

Barnes, Jeff, 1958–
     The Great Plains guide to Buffalo Billl : forts, fights & other sites /
Jeff Barnes. — First edition.
          pages   cm
     ISBN 978-0-8117-1293-4
     1. Buffalo Bill, 1846–1917. 2. Buffalo Bill, 1846–1917—Homes and
haunts—Guidebooks. 3. Frontier and pioneer life—West (U.S.) 4. Great
Plains—Guidebooks. I. Title.
F594.B94B37 2014
978'.02092—dc23
[B]
                                                            2013035260

Contents

Acknowledgments   vii
Introduction   xi

The Codys Come to Iowa   1
The Move to Kansas   7
Shipping on the Plains   14
The Pony Express and Will Cody   27
Cody in the Civil War   38
Scouting the Southern Plains   43
Bill and the Buffalo   55
A Home at Fort McPherson   63
The Battle of Summit Springs   70
Cody and the Great Buffalo Hunts   78
The Royal Buffalo Hunt of 1872   87
A Taste of Fame   94
The Road to Warbonnet   100
Last Days as a Scout   115
The Impresario Rancher   126
North Platte: Home on the Plains   132
The Birth of the Wild West   144
On to Omaha   150
Buffalo Bill's Wild West   157
Fort Yates and the Rescue of Sitting Bull   166
Wounded Knee   172
Buffalo Bill Goes to Wyoming   178
Denver and the End of the Trail   192
Remembering Buffalo Bill   201

Appendix: Quotations of William F. Cody   205
Bibliography   212
Index   217

Acknowledgments

A book like this is truly a labor of love. I'm an independent historical traveler, which means I don't get paid by a university, by government grant, or by other sources to do the research and write the book. That is not to say I don't owe thanks to the many people who gave freely of their time, knowledge, resources, and other assistance in getting this completed.

As always, my thanks first and foremost go to my wife, Susan, for her love, her patience, and her budgeting. It would be better for the bottom line if I focused entirely on freelancing or going back to the salaried world, but she knows that when I get an idea I don't usually let it drop. I love her for letting me see this one through.

I don't take on many close friends, but Paul Hedren has become one of my best in the past few years. It's wonderful to have someone who not only speaks the same language as you, but also gives of his experience, his council, and his insight. I trusted him for a thorough, honest review of the manuscript, which he gave and made it much better. Thank you, Paul!

Steve Friesen of the Buffalo Bill Museum and Dr. John Rumm of the Buffalo Bill Center of the West both gave of their experience and their review. There were nuances of Bill that wouldn't have seen the light of day in this book if not for them, and I am appreciative.

Thomas Martens of Columbus came to one of my presentations a couple of years ago, and in speaking with him after the talk I soon realized that I would have to call on him if I ever did a Buffalo Bill book. As a denizen of the birthplace of Buffalo Bill's Wild West, "Buffalo Tom" is an inveterate collector of knowledge and ephemera of William F. Cody and a great tour guide. He made this book "one of a kind" as much as anyone and he has my gratitude forever.

It's always an added treat when you can involve someone you've known for years in your current projects, and that someone was Jeff DeYoung. We both wrote for the *Nebraska City News-Press* years ago, and as Jeff currently lives and writes in Iowa and had an assignment that took him to LeClaire,

I had a trusted friend who was able to get wonderful photos for me. Thanks, Jeff!

My continued appreciation to my editor at Stackpole Books, Kyle Weaver. I'm sorry to say we've never met in person over the past six years, but the phone, e-mail, and snail-mail communication has helped to ensure a close collegial relationship. I couldn't ask for a better editor.

Michael Darby, one of the owners of the Irma Hotel in Cody, was a fantastic guide to one of the most important sites on the Buffalo Bill Trail. It's always a coin flip when you pop in unexpected to sites and hope for an interview, but Mike freely gave his time and shared the stories of the property. The restoration at the Irma Hotel shows a true love of the West and the legacy of Buffalo Bill.

I was blessed by the hospitality of Gary Ice, who took me through his home—*the* home where Cody died in Denver. This was an instance when I gave less than a day's notice that I'd be in town to someone who didn't know me at all. I was an inconvenience, no doubt about it, but Gary shared his home and the stories gladly, and I am grateful.

In the museum and attractions community, I've been helped greatly by Thomas Buecker and Jim Potter of the Nebraska State Historical Society; Phil and Sharleen Wurm and the Decatur County Last Indian Raid Museum; Don Westfall of the Ellis County (Kansas) Historical Society; Chuck Henline at Fort Cody in North Platte; Thomas Labedz of the University of Nebraska State Museum; Patricia Norman of the Trailside Museum at Fort Robinson; Lori Bitney at the Irma Hotel; Susan Krueger of the Colorado State Capitol; Samantha Hopkinson at the Buffalo Bill Ranch State Park of North Platte; Patricia LaBounty of the Union Pacific Museum; and Bob Schiffke of the Buffalo Bill Museum in LeClaire. Thanks to my friend Layton Hooper for his good Kansas research.

I have some wonderful friends who helped to keep the gas tank full along the way, too. Bev Johns and Howard and Joan Hunter have been great supporters, as has Krystal "KJ" Steward, and I've also been blessed to have John Bryan, Russ Gifford, John Richardson, Darryl Willard, and Terri Zapata in my corner. Thank you, all!

My thanks to Linda Hein, now retired from the Nebraska State Historical Society Archives—I'm going to miss her greatly on the next research trip. While speaking of the NSHS, let me express my appreciation to Mike Smith and the staff at the society, as well as to fellow members of the board of trustees. My thanks also go out to my fellow members of the Omaha Westerners for their continued support.

Thanks also to friend Doug Scott and to archivist Laura Jowdy of the Congressional Medal of Honor Society for their insight into Cody's medal of 1872. Doug's assistance on the Royal Buffalo Hunt of 1872 was also invaluable. I must also express my appreciation to Gary Rosenberg at the Douglas County Historical Society for tracking down Cody in Omaha.

I want to also thank Bill and Jody Holly of the Big Bear Motel in Cody; Todd W. Trofholz of Glur's Tavern in Columbus; and John Mintling, Jeff Alden, Kaycee Anderson, Joe Becker, Scott Mueller, Patti Simpson, Kristi Kreuscher, and Debra Faulkner of the Brown Palace Hotel in Denver. Your guidance and hospitality won't be forgotten!

I don't say this enough, but thanks to my brother Alan for keeping the wheels turning on my PT Cruiser, "Barnum." This line of work racks up the miles on the cars, so he deserves all the credit for keeping me in the field.

Finally, thanks to Tony Kornheiser and the "Middles" for the company on the long hauls.

I know I've likely forgotten many and my apologies for that—I'll express them personally when we meet up again on the trail.

Introduction

Following a historical travel guide on George Custer, I wanted to write another book in the same vein but wasn't sure on whom or what. There were a half-dozen ideas on my short list, and I figured I'd probably decide on one during an October 2012 speaking tour in Kansas. These trips are great for mulling over ideas and reaching conclusions, and I found my winning subject at—of all places—a Leavenworth motel. After checking into my room for the night, I found a large image of Buffalo Bill Cody hanging on the wall. The motel apparently had a "famous Leavenworth residents" theme, but I took it as a sign to get started on Cody.

The idea of a guide book on Cody always intrigued me, and I admit he was close to the top of my list of subjects. My home state of Nebraska claims him as a favorite son, as do four other states. There are plenty of historical sites, museums, and attractions to visit. For sources, there is no lack of material on Cody—his autobiography is still in print, books written about him during his life and shortly after his death can be found without difficulty, and some excellent histories were produced generations after his passing.

After a couple of months, however, I wondered what I had gotten myself into. The material was sometimes overwhelming, and it soon became a case of what to leave out. In contrast to Custer, William F. Cody grew up on the Plains and lived nearly twice as long, thus adding many more sites to visit. Compounding that was the strong element of uncertainty with some of the sites—there are many locations within the Cody legend, with some definite or possible and others improbable or impossible.

Uncertainty permeates Cody's life, from the location of his parents' graves to Cody's own gravesite. Many people told the "Buffalo Bill" story, from unauthorized dime novelists to paid-for publicists to family members to professional historians to Cody himself, and all offer elements of truth and falsehood. The stories sometimes turn Cody into a real-life Harry Paget Flashman or Jack Crabb with the improbable actions and people he encounters.

So, in finding the historic places where Buffalo Bill walked, I sometimes had to try to determine if he truly walked where it was claimed. In the end, I included many of the sites that Cody probably didn't see, but with an advisory to that effect. Cody did so much for the promotion and presentation of the West and our impressions of it today that I think those sites should be highlighted and enjoyed with the help of this book.

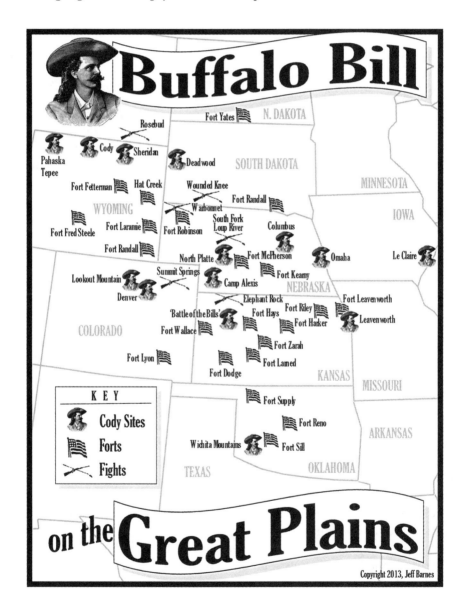

Copyright 2013, Jeff Barnes

Despite the confusion and mystery over aspects of Cody's life, he wasn't a complicated man. I think his simple goal in life was to make people happy, and he gave of himself in many ways to meet that goal. Because wealth came to him so easily, he also gave it away easily, to family, friends, acquaintances, strangers, and children. One of my favorite stories is of a visit Cody made to Omaha in 1889. He took a suite at a hotel and passed out diamond jewelry to friends, advertising in the *Omaha Herald* for any he missed to come call on him at the hotel. I loved that story, and over the course of putting together the book I came to love Cody. It's fascinating how he somewhat tripped along but continued to take the path that made him likely the most famous person in the world by the end of the nineteenth century. He was a superstar—maybe the first—and if he didn't relish the role of legend, he sure knew how to play it.

Unquestionably, the man had flaws, but that's what makes him human. It's the places and the stories they tell that keep him alive today.

Happy trails!

The Codys Come to Iowa

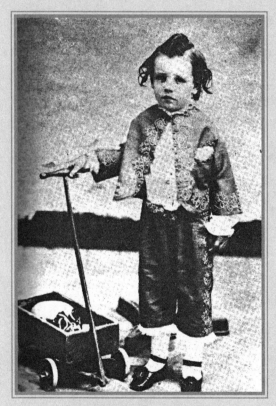

Will Cody at age four.

Isaac Cody was born outside Toronto, Canada, in 1811. His family emigrated to Ohio when Isaac was seventeen, taking up farming near Cleveland. When he was twenty-three, Isaac married Martha O'Connor, who died in 1835 while giving birth to a daughter, whom Isaac named for his wife.

A short time later, Isaac married Rebecca Sumner, who died soon after. Perhaps to leave his tragedies behind, he joined his older brother, Elijah, and his family in 1839 to help them move to Missouri. A stopover in Cincinnati while traveling down the Ohio River led to Isaac's meeting Mary Ann Bonsell Laycock and a rapid romance. After helping his brother settle in Missouri, Isaac returned to Ohio to collect his daughter and to pursue Mary; they were married in Cincinnati in 1840.

Seeking a new life for his young family, Isaac returned with them to the West, traveling down the Ohio River to the Mississippi. Finding some prosperity in trading with Indians, Isaac bought a home in the river town of LeClaire, Iowa, while also planning a new homestead to the west of town. Their son Samuel was born there in 1841, and the young family moved to the new homestead. Their first daughter, Julia, was born in 1843 at the four-room log house where the family still lived when William Frederick Cody was born on February 26, 1846.

Isaac took a position as a farm manager in 1847 to clear a six-hundred-acre piece of land near the Wapsipinicon River for William F. Brackenridge (it's not known if young Will Cody was named for him). He employed up to twenty-five men to help with the task, with some clearing the land for the farm and others quarrying stone for the large house Isaac had built on the property. (It is also not known when the Codys moved to the stone house, and it's thought Isaac and the family may have split time between it and their home near LeClaire.)

Will, or Willie as he was called by his family, showed an early penchant for close scrapes. When he was one year old, a skiff he was riding on the Mississippi took a spill; the rower was able to rescue him and four-year-old Julia. In another incident while Will was still a toddler, he narrowly missed being severely kicked by a horse, with Julia pulling him away.

Isaac, although secure in his employment and now living with his family in the stone house, decided to quit his farm manager job and join a wagon train to look for gold in California. He moved the Codys back to LeClaire in preparation for the excursion, but became ill and saw the party leave without him. Isaac instead began a stagecoach operation, hauling passengers and mail between Davenport, Iowa, and Chicago once a week.

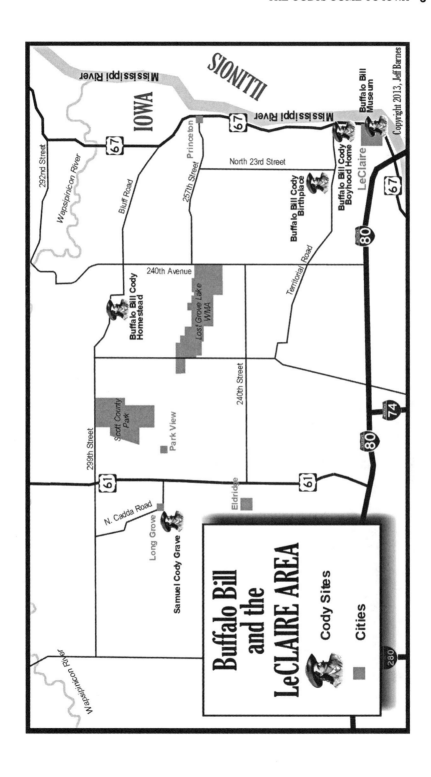

That business was sold in 1852, and Isaac again found farm management work for Brackenridge, this time in Walnut Grove near Long Grove. It was while living there in the fall of 1853 that the Cody family was hit by tragedy: the eldest son, Sam, twelve at the time, was thrown by a horse, which rolled on top of him. He died within a few days.

The loss of Sam was enough for Isaac to again pull up stakes. Elijah Cody was now living with his family in Weston, Missouri, and encouraged his younger brother to move to the West. Isaac was particularly interested in what lay across the Missouri River from Weston—the town of Leavenworth. In April 1854 the Codys moved from Walnut Grove back to LeClaire for a few days before striking out for what would soon become the new territory of Kansas.

The Trail Today

Situated north of the Quad Cities (Davenport and Bettendorf in Iowa, Rock Island and Moline in Illinois), LeClaire features great views of the Mississippi River and some interesting attractions in and around the town.

In pursuit of Buffalo Bill, the first stop should be the **Buffalo Bill Museum** in downtown LeClaire. You'll come away knowing more about the

Cody's boyhood home, which formerly stood outside of LeClaire. This was presumably occupied by his family while his father built the homestead near Princeton. The structure was purchased by the Chicago, Burlington, and Quincy Railroad and transferred for display in Cody, Wyoming, where it is now exhibited at the Buffalo Bill Center of the West.

The Buffalo Bill Cody Homestead. JEFF DEYOUNG

town than its most famous son, but there's a small section with artifacts and displays pertaining to him and his family. Most of the museum is dedicated to the less famous who made their home in the area over the last couple of centuries, from the Sauk and Fox Indians who traded with Isaac to the riverboat pilots and pioneers. *Address:* 199 North Front Street, LeClaire, Iowa 52753. *Hours:* Open daily, Monday through Saturday, 9 A.M. to 5 P.M., and Sunday, noon to 5 P.M. The museum closes at 4 P.M. during winter months. *Admission:* Adults $5, children $1. *Phone:* (563) 289-5580. *Website:* www.buffalo billmuseumleclaire.com.

Not Cody-related but still a big draw for LeClaire is a site only about two blocks south of the museum. Here at 114½ Davenport Street is the shop of **Antique Archaeology**, the home base for the popular cable TV program *American Pickers.* Mike, Frank, and Danielle aren't always in, but drop-ins are welcome.

Back on the Cody trail, if you head north on Front Street (U.S. 67) from the museum, it eventually turns into North Cody Road and, two miles north of town, intersects with Territorial Road. On your left (west), about three-tenths of a mile before you get to Territorial Road, is an Iowa Sesquicentennial marker indicating you're at the **site of Buffalo Bill's boyhood home**, where the Codys lived from 1847 to 1853. The Chicago, Burlington,

Gravesite of William Cody's brother, Sam. JEFF DEYOUNG

and Quincy Railroad bought the home in 1933 and moved it to Cody, Wyoming, as a tourist attraction. Restored, it now stands at the Buffalo Bill Center of the West (formerly the Buffalo Bill Historical Center).

Go west on Territorial Road for 1.5 miles to the intersection with North 23rd Street. Here, on the northwest corner, is a small marker commemorating the **birthplace of Buffalo Bill** and the site of the Codys' log-cabin home.

The **Buffalo Bill Cody Homestead** isn't far from here. Continue west on Territorial Road for a little more than three miles until you reach 240th Avenue. Turn right (north), drive 6.1 miles, turn left (west) on Bluff Road, and drive for about a mile until you reach the homestead, which overlooks the Wapsipinicon River Valley and is surrounded by grazing buffalo and longhorn cattle. The stone portion of the house is the home constructed by Isaac Cody, while the wing was built by later occupants. The home has been restored and furnished to feature the living room and a bedroom. There is also a gift shop. *Address:* 28050 230th Avenue, Princeton, Iowa 52768. *Hours:* Open daily, April through October, from 9 A.M. to 5 P.M. *Admission:* Adults $2, 16 and under free. *Phone:* (563) 225-2981. *Website:* www.scottcountyiowa.com/conservation/buffalobill.

Samuel Cody's grave is in the nearby town of Long Grove at the Long Grove Church and Cemetery on the northeast corner of First Street and Cadda Road. An Iowa Sesquicentennial marker helps mark the gravesite of Buffalo Bill's older brother.

The Move to Kansas

Alexander Gardner's 1867 view of the Salt Creek Valley from Government Hill, the area selected by Cody's father for settlement. KANSAS HISTORICAL SOCIETY

The Cody family increased in number before the move to Kansas. Joining Martha, Julia, and Willie were Eliza, born in 1848; Laura Ella (sometimes called Nellie or Helen), born in 1850; and May, born in 1853.

It took the Codys about a month to reach the farm of Isaac's brother Elijah, approximately two miles outside Weston, Missouri. A few days after their arrival, Elijah had business across the Missouri River at the Pottawattamie Indian Reservation in Kansas. The brothers and their wives all decided to go, and Willie came along. Crossing through the Fort Leavenworth Military Reservation, they climbed Government Hill west of the fort to get the lay of the land. Isaac and Mary fell in love with the view of the Salt Creek Valley and decided they'd eventually settle there. This is also where eight-year-old Willie saw hundreds of shippers' wagons and met his first Indians at the nearby Kickapoo Reservation.

Isaac received permission from the fort to graze his horses in the valley, later got a contract to cut hay for the army, and then was allowed to build a temporary cabin there. The act to organize the Territory of Kansas was signed by President Franklin Pierce in May 1854; when Isaac heard about it in June, he packed up his family in Weston and moved to the cabin on June 10, claiming to be the first legal settler in Kansas.

Isaac—along with a neighboring trader and a local missionary—made plans to celebrate the Fourth of July. Because most of their neighbors were Kickapoo, Delaware, and Cherokee, the Indians were also invited. Two cattle were bought, with the settlers hosting the barbecue and giving speeches and the Indians performing war dances and holding games and horse

Leavenworth in 1858, from **Frank Leslie's Illustrated Newspaper.** KANSAS HISTORICAL SOCIETY

The attack on Isaac Cody, as depicted in his son's 1879 autobiography.

races. The seeds for his future "Wild West" extravaganzas were perhaps planted with Will Cody that day.

A community activity in which Isaac was not initially involved was the growing fight between pro-slavery and abolitionist forces over whether Kansas would enter the Union as a free or slave state. According to writings by his daughters, Isaac did not think of himself as an abolitionist, but was against blacks—free or slave—entering Kansas and said as much after being talked into making a speech on September 18, 1854. His talk enraged pro-slavery spectators to the point that he was stabbed by one of them (ironically, an employee of his brother). Isaac survived the wound, but it was said to have contributed to his death three years later. His son wrote in his 1879 autobiography that this was the first blood spilled for the cause of freedom in Kansas and instead of silencing Isaac, the stabbing compelled him to become an activist in the Free-Stater cause. Isaac also founded the town of Grasshopper Falls (today's Valley Falls), thirty-five miles west of Leavenworth, to encourage the settlement of other Free-Staters.

Some did not accept the Cody family's accounts, however. William E. Connelley, former secretary with the Kansas State Historical Society, said he personally knew Cody for thirty years and probed deeply into Isaac Cody's life, interviewing a number of pioneers who knew the father. In a 1929 letter to researcher Margaret McMann of Lincoln, Connelley concluded the senior Cody was a squatter who "moved about from place to place here in Kansas, and had no influence on the free-state cause, took no part in it, was not stabbed as has been stated, and was never mistreated in any way by border ruffians." He concluded that Isaac Cody was "just a ne'er-do-well who drifted about in Kansas." However, Don Russell's biography, *The Lives and Legends of Buffalo Bill*, cites a Liberty, Missouri, newspaper of the time reporting that "A Mr. Cody, a noisy abolitionist living near Salt Creek in Kansas Territory, was severely stabbed . . ." but in a dispute over a claim.

Whether an abolitionist or a ne'er-do-well, Isaac Cody became ill during a scarlet fever outbreak and died on March 10, 1857. Young Willie Cody was now the man of the family.

The Trail Today

There is nothing to mark the **Cody homestead site**, but you can see approximately where it stood. Take U.S. 73 northwest from Leavenworth past the U.S. Penitentiary, then take the exit for Santa Fe Trail and drive north. Following the Santa Fe Trail northwest for about four miles, you'll pass the Schwinn Produce Farm and County Road 33 before reaching overhead power lines. Look to the left (south) under the lines—on top of what's called Cody Hill was the Cody homestead.

You'll pass many buildings and homes that were standing in Leavenworth at the time of Cody's youth. Also within Leavenworth proper is a city park, **Buffalo Bill Cody Park** at Shrine Park Avenue and Limit Street.

The next chapter in Cody's life—and the next chapter in this book—includes many more sites related to his growing up in Leavenworth.

Related Sites

The Cody family's first home in the area was at the farm of Isaac's brother Elijah, located near the river town of **Weston, Missouri**. Founded in 1837, the town went through a boom period in the 1850s and was once larger than Kansas City to the south and St. Joseph to the north, until floods, fires, and the Civil War took away most of its population. The people disappeared, but they left behind a great number of antebellum homes and storefronts that line today's historic shopping district of antiques, home

The Burials of Isaac and Mary Cody

While in Leavenworth, you might want to pay your respects at the graves of Buffalo Bill's parents, Isaac and Mary Cody. Unfortunately, one can't say for certain where you'd find them.

Both were buried at Leavenworth's first cemetery, Pilot Knob Cemetery (later called Mount Aurora Cemetery), which lay atop the large wooded hill west of Leavenworth High School on Tenth Avenue. Pilot Knob/Mount Aurora was the highest hill on the edge of town, and it was expected the cemetery would service the community for many years.

The growing town soon needed to expand its water supply, however, and the high ground of Mount Aurora, which contained the right kind of rock formation to hold six million gallons of water, was targeted for Leavenworth's new reservoir. Work began on the reservoir in 1882 and at least 160 burials at Mount Aurora Cemetery were transferred to new graves at Greenwood and Mount Muncie Cemeteries.

Mary Ann Laycock Cody, around 1860.

Cody didn't believe his parents were among them. Whenever he was in Leavenworth for performances, said local undertaker James C. Davis in the *Leavenworth Times* in 1938, "he asked my father to accompany him to Pilot Knob and search for his father's grave. My father knew definitely that Buffalo Bill's father was buried there, because he himself buried him and always said the grave was near the reservoir."

John Kaufman, general manager of the Leavenworth Water Department, says he has heard stories of graves remaining around the reservoir (still serving the city after 130 years) but adds that the department has never found evidence of them.

View from Pilot Knob, site of the Mount Aurora Cemetery, by Alexander Gardner in 1867. KANSAS HISTORICAL SOCIETY

The First Territorial Capitol State Historic Site at Fort Riley contains stories of the "Bloody Kansas" conflict of Buffalo Bill's childhood.

furnishings, gifts, lodging, and restaurants. Just fifteen minutes east of Leavenworth, with walking and driving tours available, it's a fun, worthwhile day trip. *Phone:* (816) 640-2909. *Email:* Visitor@WestonMO.com. *Website:* westonmo.com

Isaac Cody links his son to the conflict over Kansas's status as a free or slave state, and there are many sites in the eastern part of the state to help explain this war of ideals.

The **First Territorial Capitol State Historic Site** at Fort Riley is one of them. This historic building—located on the Fort Riley Military Reservation within the Union Pacific Railroad's right-of-way and operated by the state historical society—played a large part in setting off the American Civil War. Although the building was the capitol for only five days in 1855, some believe the actions of the pro-slavery legislators meeting here eventually led to the Civil War. Exhibits in the restored building include the stories of the anti- and pro-slavery people of the territory, along with artifacts. *Address:* Located at Exit 301 on I-70, via Huebner Road in Fort Riley. *Hours:* Friday through Sunday, March through October, 1 to 5 P.M. (October through February by appointment). *Admission:* Suggested donation of $3 for adults and $1 for students. Children are free. *Phone:* (785) 784-5535. *Website:* www.kshs.org/first_territorial_capitol. (Fort Riley is an active U.S. Army post. All visitors are required to present identification.)

In the battle to draft a constitution to govern Kansas, delegates met at Constitution Hall in the town of Lecompton in 1857. Pro-slavery forces dominated the votes and produced a constitution that protected slavery; Kansas voters rejected it the following year, pushing the nation closer to civil war. **Constitution Hall State Historic Site**, including that historic building, contains exhibits on the people and events driving the debates. *Address:* 319 Elmore Street, Lecompton, Kansas 66050 (Exit 197 on I-70). *Hours:* Wednesday to Saturday, 9 A.M. to 5 P.M.; Sunday, 1 to 5 P.M. Closed state holidays. *Admission:* Adults $3, students $1.50, Kansas Historical Foundation members and children 5 and under admitted free. *Phone:* (785) 887-6520. *Website:* www.kshs.org/constitution_hall.

Among the peaceful abolitionists in Kansas were the Rev. Samuel Adair and his wife, Florella, who settled near the Free-Stater community of Osawatomie. Their cabin was a station on the Underground Railroad, and Florella's half-brother, the abolitionist John Brown, used this cabin as his headquarters. Despite the Battle of Osawatomie—in which Brown and 30 Free-Staters fought 250 pro-slavery militia in 1856, and which saw much of the town burned—the cabin has survived through today (albeit with the help of a stone pergola built around it in the 1920s) and is part of the **John Brown Museum State Historic Site**. The museum includes exhibits on the Adairs, Brown, and others who struggled to survive the border war, and is operated in partnership with the City of Osawatomie. *Address:* 10th & Main Streets, John Brown Memorial Park, Osawatomie, Kansas 66064. *Hours:* Tuesday through Saturday, 10 A.M. to 5 P.M. *Admission:* Adults $3, students $1.50, Kansas Historical Foundation members and children 5 and under admitted free. *Phone:* (913) 755-4384. *Website:* www.kshs.org/john_brown.

On May 19, 1858, pro-slavery men killed five Free-State men and wounded five others in a ravine that is now listed as the **Marais des Cynges Massacre State Historic Site**. The massacre, which followed earlier guerrilla warfare activities on both sides, shocked the nation and became a pivotal event in the "Bleeding Kansas" era. A few months later, John Brown came to the site and constructed a fortified cabin. Learn more about Free-Staters and Border Ruffians and their stories when you drive through this beautiful natural setting. *Address:* Four miles northeast of Trading Post, Kansas, via K 52 East. *Phone:* 913-352-8890.

Shipping on the Plains

Will Cody at age eleven, near the time he began working for Russsell, Majors and Waddell.

After his father's death, Will was needed to provide income for the family. He went to work for a neighbor by driving their ox team to Leavenworth for fifty cents a day. When that job was completed, he said he accompanied his mother during her next trip to the town with the intention of asking for work with the shipping firm of Majors and Russell.

Alexander Majors noticed the boy tugging at his mother and asked what he wanted. Cody told Majors he wanted a job. A brief interview later, Cody was hired as an express boy to run messages between town and Fort Leavenworth. He was eleven years old.

The firm soon grew into the giant shipping enterprise of Russell, Majors and Waddell, which in 1855 took a two-year contract from the U.S. government to transport military supplies to the west. As that contract concluded in 1857, troubles with the Mormons in Utah Territory caused the quartermaster at Fort Leavenworth to hire the firm to move three million pounds of supplies to troops in preparation for a possible invasion of Utah.

With fifty-nine wagon trains required for the shipment, Russell, Majors and Waddell was hiring. Will made three trips west in this time, according to Cody and his sisters, although none of their recollections match. He first carried messages between the office and the fort. When that got too boring, wagon master John Willis suggested he take over the grazing of his cattle outside Leavenworth, just eight miles from the Cody home. It provided income and allowed Will to visit his family on weekends.

Will attended some school in this time. He picked up a boyhood crush on a girl in his class, a sentiment shared by another boy. The competition came to blows one day when Will pulled a knife and stabbed his rival, creating a minor wound. Rather than face the consequences from the other boy's family, Cody took Willis's suggestion to get out of town for a while and join him on the trail to Fort Kearny in Nebraska.

This chapter of Cody's life is perhaps the most complicated and least substantiated of Cody's life. There are conflicting dates for some events and no dates for others. There are conflicting stories from those who were there and those who weren't. There are recollections posted decades after the supposed events. Some stories were clearly made up after Cody became famous, and there are stories that Cody changed over time or were reported differently by his sisters. There are even stories that Cody both accepted and denied through the years.

As the legend goes, however, Mary Cody agreed to allow her son to join the trail, and young Will Cody began his first foray into the West, likely in the spring of 1858. By Cody's own account, nothing of note happened on this trip, and there's some suggestion that his job didn't have him leaving Leavenworth but rather running messages between outgoing and incoming wagon trains. Wagon master Willis said the boy actually stopped a buffalo stampede through the wagon train, while Cody described a herd's collision with the train and the ensuing havoc but never claimed he stopped it.

The shippers' route had them traveling through northwest Kansas, across the Big Blue River and into Nebraska near the Big Sandy River. The trail continued along the Little Blue and then to the Platte River Valley ten miles east of Fort Kearny. From there the route followed the Platte and North Platte to Fort Laramie, then to South Pass, through the mountains and on to the valley of the Great Salt Lake.

Cody said he joined another trip in July 1858 after returning to Leavenworth, this one taking supplies to Fort Laramie under Lewis Simpson, a somewhat unsavory character who supposedly couldn't make a trip west without killing someone. Among the thirty-one employees of this train was a man who became a close friend—James Butler Hickok, later famous as "Wild Bill" Hickok (see the sidebar on page 17).

On this trip, the wagon train was supposedly jumped by Indians at Plum Creek, thirty-five miles west of Fort Kearny, killing three herders and running off the cattle. The wagon master ordered Will and others to escape to the fort, but while doing so, he was surprised by an Indian. Will quickly shot him and made it into Fort Kearny, where a search party the next day went out and found the body. Cody said the story was in the *Leavenworth Times*, but no copies of the newspaper exist from that time.

Fort Kearny, Nebraska, in 1864.

Bill's Friend "Wild Bill"

The first time William Cody and James Hickok met, according to Cody, was when both were part of the wagon trains shipping goods west in

1857. Another member of that crew took to bullying young Billy Cody, and Hickok intervened.

"It's my business to protect that boy, or anybody else, from being unmercifully abused, kicked and cuffed, and I'll whip any man who tries it on," Cody quoted Hickok telling the bully. He was an instant fan of his rescuer, describing Hickok, who was ten years older, as "a tall, handsome, magnificently built and powerful young fellow, who could out-run, out-jump and out-fight any man on the train." When Hickok was in Leavenworth in 1859, Cody invited him and other shipping friends to stay with his family in their big house.

Cody next saw him in 1862 when Hickok returned to Leavenworth, loading and moving ox teams to Rolla, Missouri, for the federal government. Billy was talked into coming along as Hickok's assistant, and while in Missouri he got

James "Wild Bill" Hickok.

involved in betting on horse races, losing both his money and his horse. Hickok borrowed money to buy a steamboat ticket to get Cody back to Leavenworth. It was during this time in Missouri that Hickok acquired the nickname "Wild Bill." Stories of the origin differ but usually involve his taking dramatic action to break up a mob. Another version says there were two men named Hickok, one called "Wild Bill" and the other called "Tame Bill" to tell them apart.

They apparently didn't see each other again until 1866 when Cody traveled to Junction City and met with Hickok, who was then working as a scout at Fort Ellsworth and who found work for Cody doing the same. They frequently traveled together for the next few years. In 1868, a Topeka newspaper referred to Hickok and Cody delivering thieves to a local jail, with Hickok identified as "Deputy U.S. Marshal" and Cody referred to as a "government detective." Cody and Hickok continued to scout for the army and got into a fracas with a number of Mexican scouts on the campaign;

(continued on page 18)

The combination that ultimately failed: Hickok (left), Texas Jack Omohundro, and Cody.

several were shot and killed in the fight, and Cody and Hickok were sent to hunt game to keep them out of camp.

While scouting for the Fifth Cavalry in the winter of 1868–69, Cody helped rescue Hickok and a lost column, headed by Capt. William H. Penrose, that was short of supplies in Texas and the Indian Territory. Cody followed their trail easily for three days until a snowstorm hit, but still managed to locate one of Penrose's old camps and found the general's half-starved troops three days later.

Hickok had already appeared in dime novels by 1869 when Ned Buntline came to him, looking for more stories of his adventures. Not wanting the notoriety, Hickok avoided the writer, who instead tracked down Cody. When Cody entered show business in 1873, he convinced Hickok to join him—the only thing it proved was that Hickok was not meant for the stage either. He tended to drink to excess, picked fights with the audience and cast, and thought he and his fellow scouts were making fools of themselves. Hickok and Cody got into an argument while in Rochester, leading to Wild Bill's departure from the show. The two remained friends, but it was the last time they would be together.

The historical record suggests Cody and Hickok could have seen each other during the first week of July 1876, while Cody was at the Sage Creek army camp and Hickok was part of a wagon train bound for the Black Hills from Cheyenne. Given the size of the military encampment, it's likely Hickok passed through without either one realizing how close he was to the other.

According to Alexander Majors, however, only one herder was killed in this incident before the cattle were scattered. And Richard J. Walsh, in *The Making of Buffalo Bill,* said Cody frequently changed the story of killing the Indian: "Sometimes in reminiscence over a glass, Cody would say that he killed his first Indian quite accidentally. In other moods he would boast, 'I knew well

Cody never said they saw each other there, which is a shame as Hickok was shot and killed in a Deadwood poker game less than a month later.

Hickok was buried in Deadwood's Ingleside, a peaceful spot in the rapidly growing town. Within a couple of years, his remains were moved to the new Mount Moriah Cemetery. In 1906, thirty years after Hickok's death, Cody went to the graveside to pay respects to the friend of his youth.

Hickok's Trail Today

Many of the sites shared by Cody and Hickok are covered elsewhere in this guide, but the end of Hickok's trail should not be missed.

Deadwood is one of those towns that will always be identified with the Wild West. From its gold-digging roots to today's main-street casinos, Deadwood continues to bring in visitors by the thousands; its own population is less than fifteen hundred.

One of the most popular attractions continues to be **Mount Moriah Cemetery**, which overlooks the town. After parking at the gate, stop by the visitor center to pay the $1 entry fee and take in the fifteen-minute video history of the cemetery and its celebrities. Hickok's bronzed tombstone is not difficult to find once you're inside—it's just a short hike uphill before you come upon it. Next to his grave are those of Martha "Calamity Jane" Canary and Potato Creek Johnny (discoverer of a large gold nugget in the area); also explore the natural beauty of the ground and its interpretive panels. *Address:* 10 Mount Moriah Drive, Deadwood, SD 57732. *Hours:* Open daily, 8 A.M. to 8 P.M. *Phone:* (605) 578-2600.

The Black Hills' oldest history museum is Deadwood's **Adams Museum**. Its artifacts reflect the town's infamous past and powerful legends, including Wild Bill, Calamity Jane, and Deadwood Dick. Other wonderful items on exhibit include a plesiosaur, folk art collection, Lakota bead and quill work, Potato Creek Johnny's gold nugget, and N.C. Wyeth's pencil sketch drawing of Hickok. *Address:* 54 Sherman St, Deadwood, SD 57732. *Admission:* Suggested donation $5 for adults, $2 for children. *Hours:* Open daily, May to September, 9 A.M. to 5 P.M. Off-season hours vary. *Phone:* (605) 578-1714. *Website:* www.adams museumandhouse.org/

enough that in another second he would drop one of my friends, so I raised my yager and fired.' Again he would chuckle, 'That Indian has been hitched to my name like a tin kettle to a dog's tail,' and in 1914, when the Kansas historian, William E. Connelley, tried to question him about the affair, Cody changed the subject, leaving the strong suspicion that it was purely fiction."

Cody's third trip for Russell, Majors and Waddell in the fall of 1858 had him at about the Green River in the Rockies when the wagon train was attacked by militant Mormons and destroyed, forcing the group on to Fort Bridger, where they stayed for the winter. Another report has them going as far as Fort Laramie, with a side trip to supply the temporary Camp Walbach before returning to Fort Laramie for the winter.

On the return trip the next spring, with about four hundred men headed east, Simpson decided to detour around Ash Hollow and stay on the North Platte to its confluence with the South Platte for better grass. He, Cody, and the assistant wagon master were riding mules alone between the trains when they were attacked by some forty Indians. The mules were shot to use as a barricade, and the men assigned Will—then twelve—the task of felling the attacking chief, whom the boy successfully brought down.

It's possible Cody was on this trip, but there are so many improbabilities —why leave the main trail in a dangerous area with a twelve-year-old boy? why have the boy dispatch the best warrior?—that it ventures into tall tale.

Cody also reported that he had made a trip from Fort Wallace to Fort Laramie with some freighters but left them to join some trappers before returning to Leavenworth in February 1858.

Finally, Cody said a desire to tap into the Colorado gold rush led

him and others to abandon school and Leavenworth in late spring 1859 to go panning for gold. "We prospected for two months," Cody wrote, "but as none of us knew anything about mining, we met with very poor success, and . . . turned our faces eastward."

The Cody story now takes two wildly differing paths. On one, he and his friends floated down the South Platte River, wrecked at Julesburg, Colorado, and hitched a ride back to Denver and then to Leavenworth. From there, he said he went on a winter hunting expedition and killed an attacking bear with a lucky shot in the dark. His luck ran out a few days later near Prairie Dog Creek's mouth at the Republican River in Nebraska when he slipped on ice and a large stone landed on his leg and broke it.

A young and injured Will Cody encounters Indians in a dugout near Prairie Dog Creek in Nebraska.

He was forced to hole up in a dugout with supplies while his friend went for help, expecting to be gone twenty days. On the twelfth day, Will awoke to find Indians in the dugout. Incredibly, he recognized one of them from his days at Fort Laramie. This Indian, even more incredibly, was the father of Rain-in-the-Face, a Sioux to be later claimed to have killed George Custer's brother Tom at the battle of the Little Bighorn. Will used the old friendship to persuade the Indians to at least leave him the barest of essentials, and he survived in the dugout until the friend arrived on the twenty-ninth day and got both of them to Leavenworth in March 1860.

That's *one* story following the Colorado mining expedition. In the second version, the gold seekers wrecked in Julesburg, and this time Cody stayed to become part of a unique American adventure—the Pony Express.

The Trail Today

On the northwest corner of Fourth and Delaware Streets in Leavenworth was the **headquarters of Russell, Majors and Waddell**, where Will began working in his youth. A historical plaque on the side of the present building commemorates the company. (This intersection saw its share of history. On the southwest corner was the opera house known as Stockton Hall, where, in December 1859, Abraham Lincoln delivered an address. This was at the time of Cody's employment across the street, although he never mentioned seeing the future president in his Kansas hometown.)

Heading east on Delaware to Second Street and toward the river, you'll enter the area of the **Leavenworth Landing**. This section of downtown was the hub of economic activity in the town from 1854 to 1870, where thousands of pioneers purchased wagons and supplies from merchants before heading west. Cody would have been a frequent visitor.

At the end of Delaware Street is the old **Union Depot**, today's Riverfront Community and Convention Center (123 South Esplanade Street). Completed in 1884, the depot wasn't here in Buffalo Bill's boyhood, but he certainly would have come through here as an adult visiting Leavenworth. The abandoned station was renovated and expanded in 1988 to create a historic setting for public lectures, community events, and public recreation and fitness facilities.

Another site of historic note at the intersection of Delaware and Esplanade, on the northwest corner, is a marker commemorating the pre–Civil War **law offices of Sherman, Ewing and McCook**. All of the principals served with distinction in the war, but certainly the best known of them was William Tecumseh Sherman, who, as commanding general of the U.S. Army, established the School of Applied Tactics for Infantry and Cavalry

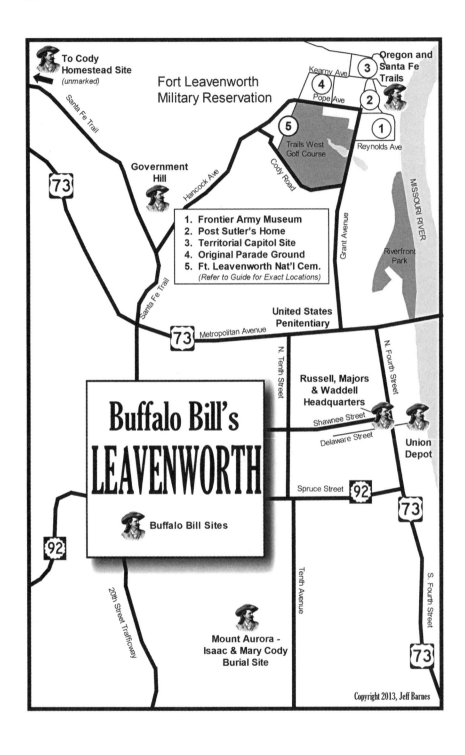

To Cody
Homestead Site
(unmarked)

Fort Leavenworth
Military Reservation

Santa Fe Trail

Kearny Ave

Pope Ave

Oregon and
Santa Fe
Trails

3

4

2

5

1

Trails West
Golf Course

Reynolds Ave

MISSOURI RIVER

Government
Hill

Hancock Ave

Cody Road

Grant Avenue

Riverfront
Park

73

1. **Frontier Army Museum**
2. **Post Sutler's Home**
3. **Territorial Capitol Site**
4. **Original Parade Ground**
5. **Ft. Leavenworth Nat'l Cem.**
   (Refer to Guide for Exact Locations)

Santa Fe Trail

United States
Penitentiary

73

Metropolitan Avenue

N. Tenth Street

N. Fourth Street

Russell, Majors
& Waddell
Headquarters

Buffalo Bill's
LEAVENWORTH

Shawnee Street

Delaware Street

Union
Depot

Spruce Street

92

73

Buffalo Bill Sites

92

20th Street Trafficway

Tenth Avenue

S. Fourth Street

Mount Aurora -
Isaac & Mary Cody
Burial Site

73

Copyright 2013, Jeff Barnes

(today's United States Army Command and General Staff College) at Fort Leavenworth.

Just south of Riverfront Community Center is the **Leavenworth Landing Park**, which tells the story of the various modes of transportation that led to the growth of Leavenworth as the major jumping-off point for the West— certainly the town's own Will Cody played a role in that development.

Fort Leavenworth abounds in historic buildings, many from the late 1800s and a few that would have stood in the 1850s when young Will Cody carried messages between his employer and the post.

After entering from the main gate on U.S. 73 (with photo ID required for post admittance), you'll pass Cody Road immediately before encountering the impressive Buffalo Soldiers memorial and statue on your right. If you don't stop to check this out, a good starting point for a tour of the post is the **Frontier Army Museum** at 100 Reynolds Avenue. The museum tells the story of the U.S. Army on the frontier and the history of Fort Leavenworth, but of special note is one of the largest collections of military carriages on exhibit (including the carriage used by Abraham Lincoln during his 1859 visit). You can also pick up a brochure for a self-guided tour of this historic post from its gift shop. *Hours:* Monday through Friday, 9 A.M. to 4 P.M.; Saturday, 10 A.M. to 4 P.M.; closed Sunday and all federal holidays. *Admission:* Free. *Phone:* (913) 684-3767. *Website:* usacac.army.mil/cac2/CSI/ FrontierArmyMuseum.asp.

From the museum, drive east on Reynolds Avenue and make a left on Sherman Avenue; follow it north until it turns into Scott Avenue. At 611 Scott Avenue is a large, wood-frame house, the **Post Sutler's Home**, built in 1841. This was built for Hiram Rich, who supplied the troops with goods like tobacco and whiskey; the structure later became the home of post commanders.

Take Scott Avenue north past the Memorial Chapel and make a right on Riverside Drive; at the bottom of the hill before you was the original boat landing of the **Oregon and Santa Fe Trails**—where Cody and his family first entered Kansas. You can still see the swale in the hillside where oxen pulled huge wagons up and out to the plains. Historical markers are located at both the top and bottom of the hill.

The 1841 Post Sutler's Home at Fort Leavenworth.

Make the loop around Riverside Drive to come back up the hill to Scott Avenue. In the parking lot, across McPherson Avenue from the old U.S. Disciplinary Barracks, was the site of the **first territorial capital of Kansas** in 1854. This building was also of note as the site of the court-martial of Lt. Col. George A. Custer in 1867.

Take McPherson Avenue west to McClellan Avenue; make a left and one block south to your left is the **Original Parade Ground**, the site selected by Col. Henry Leavenworth in 1827. Several of the buildings surrounding the parade ground were there in Cody's time, including the house at 20–22 Sumner Place, which was the quarters of post commanders from 1840 to 1890, including E. V. Sumner, Phillip St. George Cooke, and John Pope.

The Rookery, located at 12–14 Sumner Place on the northeast corner of the parade ground, was built in 1834 and is the oldest house in Kansas. When the territorial capital was at Fort Leavenworth in 1854, Gov. Andrew Reeder lived here and used an office provided by the commander of the fort. How it got the nickname "the Rookery" isn't certain, but as this was the quarters for full colonels, who wore silken eagles on their epaulettes, it's believed it came from a British term for a colony of birds.

The two similar houses to the south of the Rookery are the 1855 **Syracuse Houses**, fabricated in Syracuse, New York, and assembled at Fort Leavenworth. Custer and his wife were said to have lived in one of these houses in 1868, although some researchers say otherwise.

Related Sites

Instrumental in starting the legend of Buffalo Bill was the shipping firm that employed him, and the home of one of the firm's principals still stands for touring. The **Alexander Majors Historic House and Museum** in

Kansas City was the 1856 home of the business partner. Beautifully restored to its antebellum appearance, the home offers tours by appointment and the grounds feature blacksmithing demonstrations, gardens, and displays of tools, wagons, and carriages from the mid-1800s. *Address:* 8201 State Line Road,

The Old Freighters Museum in Nebraska City.

Legend has it that this south-central Nebraska limestone overhang was Buffalo Bill's Cave. This photo was taken around 1910.

Kansas City, Missouri 64114. *Phone:* (816) 444-1858. *Email:* coordinator@wornallhouse.org. *Website:* www.alexandermajors.com.

In the Missouri River town of Nebraska City, Nebraska, about two hours north of Leavenworth, is the **Old Freighters Museum**, originally built in 1858 as a residence by the U.S. government for one of its quartermasters, then sold in 1859 to Russell, Majors and Waddell to become their new headquarters. Nebraska City was one of the major shipping points on the Missouri, with the company sending thousands of tons of shipments through here. The restored three-story, wood-frame building now interprets the freighting and emigration years of the town. *Address:* 407 North 14th Street, Nebraska City, Nebraska 68410. *Hours:* Summer (Arbor Day through October), Friday through Sunday, noon to 4 P.M.; winter, appointment only by calling (402) 873-6188 or (402) 873-9360. *Admission:* Adults $2, children $1. *Website:* www.nebraskacitymuseums.org

If the legend is true about Cody breaking his leg while trapping and holing up in a dugout on Prairie Dog Creek to wait for help, it's believed that campsite had been found. Cody called it a dugout, but it has been known since its discovery as **Buffalo Bill's Cave**, a limestone overhang south of the Harlan County Reservoir in south-central Nebraska, north of the Kansas border. There's quite a bit to discourage a visit to the unmarked site on U.S. Army Corps of Engineers property. You'll have to drive down dirt roads to get to a spot large enough to park, then hike the half mile over hill and dale to reach the site. Once there—*if* you find it—the campsite is almost completely overgrown. And then there's the fact that it's not conclusively known Cody was there.

If you do want to make the effort, check in at the Corps office in Republican City, north of the Harlan County Dam; they'll provide you with a map of the reservoir environs and give you a fair idea of how to reach the site. *Address:* 70788 Corp Road A, Republican City, Nebraska 68971. *Phone:* (308) 799-2105. *Website:* www.nwk.usace.army.mil.

Out on the Nebraska plains, south of the Platte River, is one of the most historic sites along the westward migration and shipping trails. Fort Kearny served the routes through 1871 until no longer needed, with its reservation

Original army wagons before a reconstructed blacksmith shop at Fort Kearny State Historical Park.

then opened to homesteading. The original grounds were acquired in the 1920s and turned over to the state of Nebraska for use as a park. Today's **Fort Kearny State Historical Park** includes several reconstructions: the blacksmith shop, the earthen powder magazine, and Fort Mitchel, a stockaded post built during the 1864–65 Indian fears. The main attraction is the visitor center with its video on the fort's history, numerous artifact displays, and a series of dioramas showing the evolution of the fort. *Address:* 1020 V Road, Kearney, Nebraska 68847. *Hours:* Grounds open from dawn to dusk; visitor center and buildings open daily from March through mid-September, 9 A.M. to 5 P.M. From April 11 to May 20, during the Sand Hill cranes' migration, contact the Crane Information Center for visitation, which is then by appointment only or at the superintendent's discretion. *Admission:* Adults (13 and over) $2, children (3 to 12) $1, children under 2 free. *Phone:* (308) 865-5305. *Website:* www.outdoornebraska.ne .gov/Parks/permits/parks_historical.asp.

Another anticipated stop on the Overland Trail in Nebraska was Ash Hollow, which offered sweet spring water and tree-shaded slopes; prehistoric Indians used it, too. The history, archaeology, and paleontology of the area are interpreted at the **Ash Hollow State Historical Park** visitor center, along with the Ash Hollow Cave, exhibits, and structures. Ruts etched by westbound wagons are visible on the bluffs at nearby Windlass Hill. *Address:* P.O. Box 70, Lewellen, Nebraska 69147. *Hours:* Visitor center, May 26 to September 3, Friday through Sunday, 9 A.M. to 4 P.M. (closed Monday through Thursday); park grounds, 8 A.M. to 5 P.M. (closed November 1 to March 1). *Admission:* Adults (13 and over) $2, children (3 to 12) $1, children under 2 free. *Phone:* (308) 778-8651. *Website:* www.outdoornebraska.ne .gov/Parks/permits/parks_historical.asp.

The Pony Express and Will Cody

William Henry Jackson's depiction of Three Crossings Station, one of several Pony Express stations said to have been on young Cody's route.

For as long as Americans had occupied the West coast, communication between it and the East was needed. Commerce, politics, the military—all relied on getting information to and from the respective coasts. Doing so required weeks and sometime months of travel via overland or overseas shipping routes. With neither telegraph nor rail to link the coasts, an express route by horse was the only option for connecting the two within days. The concept of rapid communication by horseback over hundreds of miles was not new and was used sporadically throughout history. But to offer it to anyone other than kings and generals, and on a regularly scheduled route, was incredible.

Young Will Cody's hometown employer, Russell, Majors and Waddell, made that plunge into incredulity. Seeking to recoup tremendous losses taken in shipping contracts with the government, William Russell decided to pursue a lucrative mail subsidy by establishing a "pony express" between St. Joseph, Missouri, and Sacramento, California. For the seemingly profitable rate of $5 per half ounce, the new service would deliver mail between the Missouri and the Pacific within ten days.

Russell announced the Pony Express would begin on April 3, 1860, giving his company barely two months to establish nearly two hundred stations, buy hundreds of horses, and hire scores of young men as carriers. Ideally, these men would be around twenty years old, weigh about 125 pounds, and have exceptional strength and character. Fitting some of those qualifications was fourteen-year-old Will Cody.

Giving up on panning for gold in Colorado in 1859, Cody and his companions constructed a raft which they used to float down the South Platte River from Denver. The craft ran aground near Julesburg, Colorado, and the party walked into town, where Cody met "Old Jules"—Rene Jules (or Jules Reni)—an agent of the new Pony Express line and the man for whom Julesburg was named. Looking for funds (and probably adventure), Cody was hired as a rider and given a short route of forty-five miles. He stuck with the Express for two months before getting word of his mother's illness, prompting his return to Leavenworth.

After her recovery, Cody had plans to join another wagon train west from nearby Atchison, Kansas, to Fort Laramie. In that summer of 1860 in Atchison, he met up with his old employer William Russell, who gave him a letter to deliver to the notorious Jack Slade at Horseshoe Station. Slade, who headed the Pony Express division from Julesburg to Rocky Ridge and was one of the most feared men of the West, gave Cody a route from the station at Red Buttes to Three Crossings.

While employed in this section of the Nebraska Territory (now Wyoming), Cody made one of the most spectacular rides in Pony Express history. He had just completed his westbound run to Three Crossings when he found the next rider had been killed in a drunken brawl the night before. Without hesitation, Cody took the route and rode on to Rocky Ridge, where he picked up the eastbound mail and made the return trip to Red Buttes—a total distance of 384 miles, 4 miles longer than the previous record. (This distance was claimed by publicists, never by Cody, who later adjusted it to 322 miles.)

The adventures didn't end there. In his original autobiography, Cody said he was one day surprised by a party of Indians on the route. They fired on him repeatedly in the chase. He outran them, but found the station manager killed and the livestock driven off at the next stop. Undeterred, he spurred his horse on to the next station, a twenty-four-mile run on the same horse. In another incident, he arrived at a station to find a buffalo bull charging and just about to crush a three-year-old girl; he shot and killed the animal in the nick of time.

Or so go the stories attributed to Buffalo Bill in his time with the Pony Express. Discrepancies abound in the tales, beginning with when he started. Cody said it was 1859 when he ran aground near Julesburg. Unfortunately for the story, the Express began the following year.

Most of the records of Russell, Majors and Waddell relating to the Pony Express haven't survived, and for that reason and others—including the fact that none of the stories relating to Cody and the Pony Express were told until he became a public figure and press agents established him as "the hero of the plains" —there are some doubts about whether Cody actually *was* a rider. Most of the detractors say that at age fourteen or fifteen he was far too young to be hired, especially for work in some of the most dangerous country of the route. Luther North of the famed North Brothers, a longtime Cody associate, said he also applied to ride for the Pony Express and was turned down because of his age, which was the same as Cody's.

Of course, with several trips west already under his belt with the freight wagons, young Will Cody was probably more experienced than most boys his age or older. His aptitude certainly was known by the company principals who had employed him in Leavenworth, the hometown of both the firm and the boy.

Many biographies about Cody, including those by his sisters, report his Pony Express career as a matter of fact. In a book ghostwritten for Alexander Majors, the former employer wrote that Buffalo Bill was one of the most well-known and daring riders of the Pony Express. That would seem to confirm that Cody was a Pony Express rider, although the book promoted

Cody and former Pony Express rider Charles Cliff were special guests for the dedication of the Pony Express monument in St. Joseph. BUFFALO BILL MUSEUM/CITY AND COUNTY OF DENVER

Buffalo Bill's Wild West and was dedicated to Cody, who wrote the preface and paid for its publication. To be fair, Majors did ask that blatant exaggerations be eliminated from the book.

The job that Cody did have on horseback for Russell, Majors and Waddell was running mail from Leavenworth to St. Joseph, but this was not the established route of the Express. The historian Connelley said that Cody admitted he never rode *the* Pony Express and that Majors confirmed it.

The fact remains that few people would know about the Pony Express today without Buffalo Bill. Cody made the Pony Express a key component of his Wild West presentations, reenacting the rides and telling their stories of adventure before millions. If not a rider, he was certainly the protector and promoter of its memory—and that might be enough to make him the greatest member of the Pony Express of all.

The Trail Today

Following the Pony Express route through the Great Plains, you'll find a rich trail of reminders of this exciting chapter in American history.

Starting in downtown St. Joseph, Missouri—birthplace of the Pony Express—you'll find an heroic-sized bronze statue of horse and rider at

Tenth and Frederick Streets. The two-ton statue by Hermon A. MacNeil was installed in 1938.

The **Patee House Museum**, built in 1858 as a 140-room luxury hotel, was the headquarters for the Express during its years of operation. It was one of the best-known hotels west of the Mississippi during Cody's time and is known today as an award-winning museum of the Old West. The Patee (pronounced *PAY-tee*) House features two floors of exhibits touching on many aspects of the West, including an 1860 train, an 1877 railroad depot, a stagecoach, a carousel, wagons, buggies, carriages, hearses, a blacksmith shop, model railroads, a gallery of Western art, and an actual gallows. Adjacent to the museum is the home where Jesse James was shot and killed by Robert Ford (after his death, the James family stayed and were interviewed in the hotel). *Address:* 1202 Penn Street, St. Joseph, Missouri 64503. *Hours:* Monday through Saturday, 10 A.M. to 4 P.M.; Sunday, 1 to 4 P.M. (November through February, open weekends only). *Admission:* Adults $6, seniors (over 60) $5, students $3, children 5 and under free. *Website:* www.ponyexpress jessejames.com.

Three blocks to the east of the Patee House Museum is a second museum in an historic structure. The former Pikes Peak Stables launched the first rider of the Pony Express and today they fittingly house the **Pony Express National Museum**. Where horses and mules were once stabled,

The Pony Express National Museum in St. Joseph, Missouri.

visitors now learn the whole story of the express mail service through interactive exhibits, displays, and artifacts. Across the street in Patee Park is a large stone monument installed by the Daughters of the American Revolution to honor the Pony Express; Buffalo Bill was present for its dedication in 1912. *Address:* 914 Penn Street, St. Joseph, Missouri 64503. *Hours:* November to February, Monday to Saturday, 9 A.M. to 4 P.M., Sunday, 11 A.M. to 4 P.M.; March to October, Monday to Saturday, 9 A.M. to 5 P.M., Sunday, 11 A.M. to 4 P.M. *Admission:* Adults $6, seniors over sixty $5, students $3, children six and under free. *Phone:* (816) 279-5059. *Website:* www.ponyexpress.org.

Farther west on the route, in the northeastern Kansas town of Marysville, is the stone **Pony Express Barn**. This structure was built in 1859 and contracted to Russell, Majors and Waddell in 1860 as a livery stable for the Pony Express–Home Station No. 1, where the first rider from St. Joseph would change out for a fresh rider. This stable now serves as a museum operated by the chamber of commerce. *Address:* 106 South Eighth Street, Marysville, Kansas 66508. *Hours:* Monday to Saturday, 9 A.M. to 4 P.M., Sunday, noon to 4 P.M. *Admission:* Free. *Phone:* (785) 562-3825. *Website:* www .marysvillekansaschamber.org.

Two miles east of Hanover, Kansas, on SR243, **Hollenberg Pony Express Station State Historic Site** is the only unaltered Pony Express station remaining in its original location. This most westerly Pony Express station

An original Pony Express station, located in Gothenburg, Nebraska.

in Kansas—123 miles west of St. Joseph—was built by Gerat H. Hollenberg in 1857 or 1858. It became his family home, a neighborhood store, a tavern, a stage station for the Overland Express, and in 1860 a station for the Pony Express. *Address:* 2889 23rd Road, Hanover, Kansas 66945 (four miles north of U.S. 36 on K-148, one mile east of Hanover on K-243). *Hours:* April through September, Wednesday and Sunday, 1 to 4 P.M.; Thursday through Saturday, 10 A.M. to 5 P.M. *Admission:* Free. *Phone:* (785) 337-2635. *Website:* www.kshs.org/p/hollenberg-pony-express-station-about/15878.

Across the border in Nebraska, Rock Creek Station was originally established along the Oregon–California Trail in 1858 to sell supplies and other services to the emigrants. The station subsequently served as a relay station for the Pony Express and finally as a stage station for the Overland stage. This was the site of a well-known incident in 1861 in which Cody's friend "Wild Bill" Hickok shot and killed the owner of the station. The **Rock Creek Station State Historical Park** includes reconstructed buildings and a museum. *Address:* 57426 710 Road, Fairbury, Nebraska 68352. *Hours:* Daily, 9 A.M. to 5 P.M. (summer); weekends only, 1 to 5 P.M. (winter). *Admission:* Adults (13 and over) $2, children (3 to 12) $1, children under 2 free. *Phone:* (402) 729-5777. *Website:* www.outdoornebraska.ne.gov/Parks/permits/parks_historical.asp.

Original Pony Express stations stand today in the city parks of Cozad and Gothenburg, both moved from their original sites. The Gothenburg one includes a small museum, gift shop, and visitor information. *Address:* 1500 Lake Avenue, Gothenburg, Nebraska 69138. *Hours:* Weekdays, 8 A.M. to 8 P.M. (summer); 9 A.M. to 6 P.M. (May and September); 9 A.M. to 3 P.M. (April and October). *Admission:* Free. *Phone:* (308) 537-3505.

One of the most familiar landmarks on the Pony Express and other trails was Chimney Rock, the first of several sandstone outcroppings that appeared as emigrants entered the High Plains. The jutting "smokestack" of the rock has eroded somewhat over the years, but it still casts a dramatic appearance at **Chimney Rock State Historic Site**. A modern visitor center, administered by the Nebraska State Historical Society, presents the history of the landmark through a short film, displays, artifacts, and photographs; an excellent gift and bookshop provides even more information on the historic routes. *Address:* Bayard, Nebraska 69334 (1.5 miles south of Highway 92 on Chimney Rock Road). *Hours:* Open daily, 9 A.M. to 5 P.M.; open Memorial Day, Fourth of July, and Labor Day, but closed all state holidays in the off-season. *Admission:* Adults $3, children with adults and NSHS members free. *Phone:* (308) 586-2581. *Website:* www.nebraskahistory.org/sites/rock/.

The landmark that emigrant diaries mentioned the most after Chimney Rock was Scotts Bluff, a huge sandstone outcropping south of the

The most-recognized landmark of the Pony Express, as well as the Oregon, Mormon, California and Overland trails, was Nebraska's Chimney Rock.

North Platte River. The **Scotts Bluff National Monument** today relates the history of the landmark and nearby Mitchell Pass, a spectacular drive to the top of the bluff, and the nation's biggest and best collection of William Henry Jackson paintings. Jackson, following service in the Union army during the Civil War, was hired as a bullwhacker for a freighting outfit bound for the gold mines of Montana. Along the old Oregon Trail, he sketched the sights and people he saw, including those associated with the Pony Express. Following a career that established him as one of the greatest photographers of the American West, Jackson—then in his nineties—began painting from his sketches. A wing of the visitor center at Scotts Bluff National Monument is dedicated to his life and work, and more than sixty of his original paintings are a part of the park's collection. *Address:* 190276 Old Oregon Trail, Gering, Nebraska 69341 (three miles west of Gering on State Highway 92 West). *Hours:* Open daily, except January 1, Martin Luther

King Day, Presidents Day, Thanksgiving, and Christmas. Open 9 A.M. to 5 P.M. in summer, 9 A.M. to noon and 1 to 5 P.M. in winter. *Admission:* Hikers, bicyclists, and motorcycles $3; vehicles $5. *Phone:* (308) 436-9700. *Website:* www.nps.gov/scbl.

Overlooking the city of Casper, Wyoming, the **National Historic Trails Interpretive Center** tells the story of the Pony Express, Oregon, California, and Mormon trails that passed through this part of the county. Developed as a partnership between the city, the Bureau of Land Management (BLM), and the National Historic Trails Center Foundation, it interprets the role of the trails throughout U.S. history with interactive exhibits and videos. *Address:* 1501 North Poplar Street, Casper, Wyoming 82601 (I-25 at Exit 189). *Hours:* Open daily, 8 A.M. to 5 P.M. from May through August; open 9 A.M. to 4:30 P.M. in non-peak months; closed Sunday and Monday. *Admission:* Ranges from $4 to $6, with youth 16 and under free. *Phone:* (307) 261-7780. *Website:* http://www.blm.gov/wy/st/en/NHTIC.html.

Although Fort Caspar was not in existence at the time of the Pony Express (it was established a year after the Express ended), its site was the location of the Platte Bridge Station. A marker commemorates that station at **Fort Caspar Museum and Historic Site**, an excellent city-owned museum that tells the story of the post and the events surrounding it. The reconstructed fort was built on its original site from plans left by Lt. Caspar

Riders passed through Platte Bridge Station, later the site of Fort Caspar. The fort was reconstructed on its original site by the city of Casper, Wyoming.

Split Rock, visible in the background, overlooks the site of the Split Rock Station—one of the claimed stops for Cody's Pony Express career.

Collins, who was killed while protecting a supply train from Indian attack and for whom the post was named. The site includes tours, a bookstore, gift shop, restrooms, and a picnic area. *Address:* 4001 Fort Caspar Road, Casper, Wyoming 82604. *Hours:* Tuesday through Saturday, 8 A.M. to 5 P.M.; closed Sunday and Monday. *Admission:* Adults $3, teens (13 to 18) $2, children 12 and under free. *Phone:* (307) 235-8462. *Website:* www.fortcaspar wyoming.com.

You can follow Buffalo Bill's historic Pony Express route for the most part by taking Wyoming 220 southwest from Casper. His route began at the next station ten miles west of the Platte Bridge, the Red Buttes Station. There's no marker, but the station stood about two hundred feet southwest of the Oregon Trail marker.

Willow Springs, Horse Creek, and Sweetwater Stations followed as the trail approached **Independence Rock**, which is impossible to miss along 220. This huge, rounded mass of granite was one of the most famous and sought-after landmarks along the trails, and many emigrants paused not only to drink from the cool Sweetwater River, but also to carve their names into the side of the mount. "The Great Register of the Desert" is now a modern highway rest area, continuing the tradition begun along the trail. Independence Rock is located fifty-five miles southwest of Casper on Wyoming 220.

The Devil's Gate Station was named for the noted cleft (370 feet high, 1,500 feet long) in the east end of the Sweetwater Rocks, six miles farther southwest on 220. Many emigrants walked and waded through the canyon in the cooling Sweetwater, while their wagons (and the Pony Express) followed the dusty trail through the pass to the east. A BLM interpretive site is located just south of the Gate, giving details of the long and colorful history of the area.

The next stop was made at Plant's before the final station on his regular route, **Split Rock**, the dominant landmark of the Sweetwater Valley. Its "gun sight" notch profile was visible to emigrants a day before they reached it from the east, and two days after they passed. Split Rock itself is located in Natrona County, but a BLM interpretive rest area is located just over the county line in Fremont County. You'll turn right (north) from 220 to U.S. 287 for eight miles west of the Muddy Gap junction; the Split Rock rest area is on the north side of the highway. Another three and a half miles beyond the rest area is a historical marker turnout for Split Rock. From here, you'll get a good view of the mountain's notch from the west.

Related Events

Every June, the National Pony Express Association conducts its annual "Re-Ride of the Pony Express Trail," a 10-day, 24-hours-a-day, non-stop recreation of the 1,966-mile route. The NPEA rounds up more than 600 riders and horses for the event, which starts from St. Joseph in odd-numbered years and Sacramento in even-numbered years and sticks as close to the original route as possible. Riders carry commemorative letters with a special U.S. Postal Service cancellation in a *mochila* created for that year's ride and swapped over from horse to horse just like in 1860 and 1861.

It's exciting to see, especially at some of the more historic sites. The riders aren't there for long—do yourself a favor and arrive early at the switch-off sites to visit with the people who have turned a passion for horses and history into an annual eight-state event. Visit the NPEA at www.xphome station.com for the schedule and projected arrival times (depending on weather and other factors, they can be off by several hours).

Recommended Reading

Saddles and Spurs: The Pony Express Saga by Raymond W. Settle and Mary Lund Settle (Lincoln, NE: Bison Books, 1972); *The Saga of the Pony Express* by Joseph J. DiCerto (Missoula, MT: Mountain Press Publishing Company, 2002); *The Pony Express Trail: Yesterday and Today* by William E. Hill (Caldwell, ID: Caxton Press, 2010); *On the Winds of Destiny: A Biographical Look at Pony Express Riders* by Jacqueline Lewin and Marilyn Taylor (St. Joseph, MO: Platte Purchase Publishers, 2002); *The Pony Express from St. Joseph to Fort Laramie* by Merrill Mattes and Paul Henderson (St. Louis, MO: Patrice Press, 1989); and *The Pony Express: A Photographic History* by Bill and Jan Moeller (Missoula, MT: Mountain Press Publishing Company, 2002).

Cody in the
Civil War

Cody as a private in the Seventh Kansas Volunteer Cavalry.

Missouri was the third most fought over state (after Virginia and Tennessee) during the American Civil War, with agitation still rife along its western border after the "Bloody Kansas" years. Will Cody was fifteen when the Civil War erupted in 1861, too young to enlist but not too young to become active in the militia. He said he quit the Pony Express at Horseshoe Station and returned to Leavenworth on about June 1 of that year.

As a Free-State Kansan, Cody wrote that since Missouri was a slave state, he took it for granted that all of its inhabitants must be secessionists and therefore enemies. In large part as retaliation for the treatment he said his family had received from pro-slavery factions in the border war, he joined an independent group whose purpose was making war on Missourians. Their operations during the summer of 1861 consisted of stealing horses from certain farms under the cover of night. When Cody's mother found out about it, she immediately shamed him into quitting his "jay-hawking" activities.

Stuck in Leavenworth, Cody said that before long he ran into Wild Bill Hickok, who was there loading and moving ox teams to Rolla, Missouri, for the federal government. Young Will—often called Billy at this point—was talked into coming along as Hickok's assistant, and while in Missouri, he got involved in horse racing and lost both his money and horse in wagering. Hickok borrowed money to buy a steamboat ticket to get Cody back to Leavenworth.

For the rest of the year, Cody said he carried dispatches to Fort Larned and assisted in buying horses for the government. In the spring of 1862, he reported that he acted as a guide and scout for the Ninth Kansas Volunteers between Fort Larned and Fort Lyon along the Arkansas River/Santa Fe Trail. The regiment was involved in several small incidents, including Locust Grove in the Indian Territory (now Oklahoma). His sister Julia later wrote that Cody met Kit Carson, then colonel of the First New Mexico Volunteer Infantry, while he was in Santa Fe.

Back in Leavenworth by fall, Cody joined a home-guard organization called the Red Legged Scouts. He reported their duties as hunting the Younger brothers (the bandits later associated with Frank and Jesse James) and carrying dispatches between Fort Leavenworth, Fort Dodge, Fort Gibson, and other posts. Cody escorted a small train to Denver and arrived there in September 1863. Receiving a letter from Julia telling him their mother was dangerously ill, he returned to Leavenworth, where Mary Ann Cody died on November 22.

Billy then engaged in what he called a "dissolute and reckless life," associating with gamblers, drunks, and other unsavory types. During this time the Seventh Kansas Volunteer Cavalry came to town on furlough in February 1864. Quite a few of its members were former fellow Red Legged Scouts, and they encouraged Cody to sign up.

"I had no intention of doing anything of the kind," he wrote, "but one day, after having been under the influence of bad whisky, I awoke to find myself a soldier in the Seventh Kansas. I did not remember how or when I had enlisted, but I saw I was in for it, and that it would not do for me to endeavor to back out." Cody was mustered into service at Fort Leavenworth on February 19, 1864, as a private in Company H of the Seventh Kansas Volunteers. The official enlistment gives a description of eighteen-year-old Cody: brown eyes and hair, fair complexion, five feet, ten inches tall.

The regiment reassembled in March and moved on to St. Louis and then Memphis. They became part of a cavalry corps under Brig. Gen. Benjamin H. Grierson around the Tennessee-Mississippi border and were involved in several small engagements. Their biggest fight was the Battle of Tupelo on July 14. The Seventh engaged only the enemy's pickets that day; still, they were a victor in a rare defeat for Confederate commander Nathan Bedford Forrest.

Cody's autobiography stated that Seventh Kansas Volunteers fought or skirmished nearly daily for six weeks; however, the official army records show that his regiment took part in eight engagements, with one man killed and four wounded. His autobiography also said he was part of a scouting party that captured Maj. Gen. John S. Marmaduke, commander of Price's

cavalry, and guarded Marmaduke as he was transferred to Fort Leavenworth. Again, the records do not show he was scout or spy for the army during this time. They do show that Private Cody was detached for hospital duty in Pilot Knob in January 1865 and detailed for special duty as an orderly at St. Louis from February through September.

Cody was mustered out as a private on September 29, 1865,

Cody and Louisa Frederici in 1866 at the time of their marriage.

Louisa Frederici Cody, at about the time she married Cody.

at Fort Leavenworth. He had served one year, seven months, and ten days, missing none of the battles, campaigns, or skirmishes in which his regiment was involved during his term.

While on duty in St. Louis, Cody met Louisa Frederici, the daughter of John Frederici, an immigrant from Alsace-Lorraine, and an American-born woman whose last name was Smith. The stories vary widely on how they met. Cody says little, but "Lulu" (as he called her) said that she had mistakenly slapped him instead of a cousin who had startled her. After this abrupt meeting, she then conspired with him to pretend they were engaged in order to ward off one of her suitors. Cody liked her enough to become a regular suitor himself, and following his discharge in Leavenworth in September 1865, he went back to St. Louis to reaffirm his sentiments to Louisa, who agreed to marry him.

With Louisa's acceptance in hand, he returned to Kansas to make some money. He drove a string of horses from Leavenworth to Fort Kearny in the Nebraska Territory, and once there was hired to run a stagecoach between Fort Kearny and Plum Creek. More than twenty years later, Cody claimed that during this time he had been a dispatch rider and guide for Gen. William Tecumseh Sherman. When Cody asked for a testimonial from him in 1887, the general wrote that Bill had "guided me honestly and faithfully, in 1865–66, from Fort Riley to Kearny, in Kansas and Nebraska." Sherman undoubtedly confused him with Wild Bill Hickok, who did serve Sherman in that capacity. Not one to let a good reference get away, Cody and his promoters allowed Sherman's statement to stand, and a new Buffalo Bill story was built around it.

Cody ran the route until February 1866, when he decided that settling down in marriage was a better alternative to "bounding over the cold, dreary road day after day." He immediately left for St. Louis, and on March 6, 1866, he and Louisa were married.

On the riverboat ride back to Leavenworth, Cody claims to have been recognized from his jayhawker days by some Missouri bushwhackers. He said they telegraphed ahead to friends to have Cody pulled from the boat at Lexington, but the boat captain saw the brewing fight and pulled away from the dock before it could develop. Louisa said later she recalled a dispute on the trip, but that it didn't involve her new husband.

The Codys settled in Leavenworth, renting the house in Salt Creek Valley that had belonged to his mother. Cody tried to operate it as a hotel, the Golden Rule House, but gave it up after six months. His sister Helen said her generous and hospitable brother would cover for those arriving without money, and word got around. "Travelers . . . would go miles out of their way to put up at his tavern," she wrote. "Socially he was an irreproachable landlord; financially his shortcomings were deplorable."

The time had come for Cody to make a change in his life, one that would take him to the West and alter his life forever.

Related Sites

Even if Cody saw limited action, the traveler will find several Civil War hot spots around his hometown of Leavenworth.

One of the largest—the one with the most history still in place—is the **Battle of Lexington State Historic Site**, which highlights the 1861 fight between Col. James Mulligan's Union forces and Gen. Sterling Price's Confederate Missouri State Guard. (It is sometimes called the "Battle of the Hemp Bales" since Rebel forces used them as mobile breastworks to advance on the Union's hilltop position, which fell to Price's men.) The open hill and orchard remain, and guided tours are offered and include the Anderson House with its bullet holes and evidence of cannon shots. (Be sure to visit the courthouse in town where a cannonball is still embedded in one of its columns.) A visitor center provides a comprehensive view of the battle. *Address:* 1101 Delaware Street, Lexington, Missouri 64067 (twenty miles north of I-70 from exit 49 on Missouri 13). *Hours:* Monday to Saturday, 9 A.M. to 5 P.M.; Sunday, 10 A.M. to 6 P.M. (9 A.M. to 5 P.M. in the off-season). (Visit the website for visitor center and Anderson House hours.) *Admission:* Free (there is a charge for the Anderson House tour). *Phone:* (660) 259-4654. *Website:* mostateparks.com/park/battle-lexington-state-historic-site.

Suggested Reading

The Civil War in the American West by Alvin M. Josephy Jr. (Vintage Books, 1993); *Civil War on the Western Border, 1854–1865* by Jay Monaghan (University of Nebraska Press, 1984); and *Civil War on the Missouri-Kansas Border* by Donald L. Gilmore (Pelican Publishing Company, 2005).

Scouting the Southern Plains

William Cody as a scout from 1870.
SMITHSONIAN INSTITUTION

Ill too soon Cody realized domestic life didn't suit him. Longing to return to the West, he decided to sell the Golden Rule House and leave his wife behind while searching for income and a future for them. Louisa first stayed with his sister Helen in Leavenworth and later moved back to St. Louis and her family.

In late 1866, Cody traveled to Junction City near Fort Riley and again met with Wild Bill Hickok, who was working as a scout at Fort Ellsworth and found work for Cody doing the same. Cody returned briefly to Louisa for the birth of their daughter, Arta, on December 16.

As a scout, Cody was assigned to know the areas that the army didn't. Scouts were used to find trails, guide columns, and carry messages from one command to another. Their purpose was not to fight Indians, although they sometimes did. Scouts were fairly well paid for their service, at least by army standards, ranging from sixty to one hundred and fifty dollars a month, which reflected the temporary nature of their jobs but also the hazards.

Cody said he first met George Armstrong Custer while working out of Fort Harker and the original Fort Hays. The Seventh Cavalry commander needed a guide to take him from Hays to Fort Larned, wrote Cody in his autobiography, and was so pleased with Cody's service that he offered him employment should he ever need it.

The facts don't quite support that, however. Custer went from Fort Larned to Fort Hays in April 1867, and the records don't show that he returned. Nor is Cody among the Kansas scouts mentioned by Custer in his memoir, *My Life on the Plains*, although that may have been an intentional oversight (see page 109).

There is also conflicting information from Cody about his time at Fort Hays. He said was here in June 1867 when a flash flood on Big Creek nearly destroyed the fort, prompting its move fourteen miles northwest. He also wrote he was scouting for Custer in June as he and the Seventh passed through the sand hills of the Smokey Hill River. Custer was on the trail when the flood hit, so Cody was either at the flood or on the march, but not both (and possibly neither).

While at the new Fort Hays, Cody was sent to guide and scout for a company of "Buffalo Soldiers" from the Tenth Cavalry who were responding to an Indian raid on the Kansas Pacific in which six were killed and about one hundred horses and mules were run off. They found the Indians near the Saline River on August 2, 1867. Their commander, Maj. George A. Armes, ordered their howitzer to be set up on a knoll and prepared for firing if

Bvt. Maj. George A. Armes.

necessary. As Armes crossed the river to negotiate with the Indians, another band chased off the soldiers guarding the cannon; Armes returned to run the Indians off the knoll. A sergeant was killed and Armes was wounded in continuous fighting on the way back to Fort Hays.

Some have questioned Cody's role in the fight. Col. Frank Triplett in *Conquering the Wilderness* said Cody's coolness and courage prevented the extermination of the entire command, but others questioned whether he was even there. Cody claimed higher-than-actual casualties from the fight, and Armes said only that a scout was present, but didn't name him.

Cody came back to Fort Hays and quit scouting to run dispatches between Forts Harker and Hays. He took on other tasks for income, including hunting buffalo and land speculation by founding a town (see next chapter). The *St. Louis Democrat* of February 17, 1868, mentioned a hunting party under the direction of Cody, "the noted guide." And two months later,

Depiction of the Saline River battle from George A. Armes's book, Ups and Downs of an Army Officer, *written in 1911.*

a Topeka newspaper reported that Hickok, "Deputy U.S. Marshal," and Cody, "government detective," delivered thieves to a local jail.

The movements of Cody from May to August in 1868 aren't completely clear, as he was based at several of the forts. No scouting was needed in this period, so Cody served as a guide and courier at Fort Larned for Col. William B. Hazen, superintendent of Indian affairs on the Southern Plains. Returning to the fort after escorting Hazen to Fort Zarah, Cody stated that he was captured by Indians who took him to the Kiowa chief Satanta but was able to trick the chief into releasing him.

In another incident, Cody volunteered to carry important dispatches from Larned to Gen. Phil Sheridan at Fort Hays—a run no other scout was willing to take through hostile Indian territory. He made the trek overnight, bringing Sheridan the dispatches at dawn. Sheridan had messages to send to Fort Dodge, ninety-five miles to the south. Again no scouts volunteered save for Cody, who made the run after a five-hour rest.

At Dodge, the post commander needed to send dispatches to Fort Larned. Cody volunteered, but lacking a fresh horse, he was forced to take a government mule. The mule left him when Cody stopped for water along the trail, forcing the scout to walk the last thirty-five miles to Larned. In less than sixty hours, Cody had traveled an amazing three hundred and fifty

Fort Larned in 1867. FORT LARNED NATIONAL HISTORIC SITE

Lt. Gen. Philip Sheridan.

miles, the last tenth on foot. Sheridan was duly impressed. "Such an exhibition of endurance and courage was more than enough to convince me that his services would be extremely valuable in the campaign," he later wrote, "so I retained him at Fort Hays till the battalion of the Fifth Cavalry arrived, and then made him chief of scouts for that regiment." Press agents later revised that testimony, dropping "for that regiment" from Sheridan's words. Cody was advertised in future shows as "Chief of Scouts in the U. S. Army"—more than a slight exaggeration.

Cody continued to impress the commanders while on campaign. Gen. Eugene A. Carr wrote that Cody "was the best white trailer I ever saw. On my first expedition we soon learned to understand each other. He saw that I knew the direction I wanted to go and I saw he knew how to take me there."

The Fifth was sent to Fort Wallace and then to Fort Lyon, arriving in November 1868. They were immediately sent with supplies for General Penrose, then on campaign at the Canadian River in Texas and the Indian Territory. Cody followed the trail easily for three days until a snowstorm hit, but still managed to locate an old camp of Penrose's and found the general's

Fifth Infantry Band before the officers' quarters of the new Fort Hays in 1869.

Fort Wallace in 1867, by Theodore Davis, for Harper's Weekly.

half-starved troops three days later. Carr wrote several letters praising Cody's skill in locating Penrose.

Now commanding all of the troops, Carr established a supply camp and continued the Canadian River campaign but found no Indians. The command returned to Fort Lyon in March 1869 for thirty days of rest before their next transfer to Fort McPherson on the Platte. Before the move, Cody successfully trailed and captured two horse thieves in Denver, although one escaped on the return to the fort.

There was some excitement on the way to Fort McPherson. On May 13, 1869, Cody and a scouting party found a Sioux village just a few miles south of the Kansas-Nebraska border on Beaver Creek, near a rock formation called Elephant Rock. Before they could return to the column, a hunting party found them and began an attack. Cody made it back to Carr, who brought up most of the column. The resulting fight left four men killed and three wounded; Carr reported twenty-five Indians killed and twenty wounded.

The Sioux retreated to the north and the Republican River. Cody and the Fifth Cavalry crossed into Nebraska, following the Sioux trail. On May 16, an advance guard including Cody was surrounded on Spring Creek, north of today's Oxford, Nebraska. The troops exchanged fire with their attackers for half an hour until a relief company was spotted and the Indians ran. Three soldiers were killed, and Cody very nearly joined them.

"They all, to this day, speak of Cody's coolness and bravery," Carr later wrote. "Reaching the scene we could see the Indians in retreat. A figure with apparently a red cap rose slowly up the hill . . . it was Cody without his broad-brimmed sombrero. On closer inspection I saw his head was swathed in a bloody handkerchief, which served not only as a temporary bandage, but as a chapeau—his hat having been shot off, the bullet plowing his scalp badly for about five inches. . . . (A) very close call but a lucky one." Undaunted by his close scrape, Cody volunteered to carry dispatches to Fort Kearny overnight while the column rested.

Carr mentioned Bill prominently in his official report and requested in a separate letter that his scout receive an extra one hundred dollars in bonus to his pay. The request worked its way up to the secretary of war, who authorized the bonus.

This was a recognition that no other scout could claim and rarer than a citation for the Congressional Medal of Honor (which Cody would later win) . . . yet he never mentioned this monetary award in his memoirs, nor did he mention the nearly fatal shot he received at Spring Creek.

The Trail Today

Many of the forts frequented by Buffalo Bill as a scout are marked, and some even still exist as staffed attractions.

The town of Kanopolis (once envisioned as a potential capital of Kansas) grew up around the remains of Fort Harker, and as a result, four of its 1867-built structures survived. Three of them are owned by the Ellsworth County Historical Society, the largest of which is the former guardhouse, today the **Fort Harker Museum**. The two-story sandstone building contains a number of artifacts from the fort and community, but of greatest interest to Buffalo Bill fans is a limestone tablet with the inscription "FT. HARKER-W.F.CODY-1874." There's no evidence Buffalo Bill carved this, but no evidence he didn't. *Address:* 309 West Ohio Street, Kanopolis, Kansas 67454. *Admission:* Adults $3, children $1, children 6 and under free. *Hours:* Summer (May through September), Tuesday through Saturday, 10 A.M. to 5 P.M.; Sunday, 1 to 5 P.M. Winter (November through March), Saturday, 10 A.M. to 5 P.M.; Sunday, 1 to 5 P.M. Spring and fall (April and October), Tuesday through Friday, 1 to 5 P.M.; Saturday, 10 A.M. to 5 P.M.; Sunday, 1 to 5 P.M. Closed Mondays and major holidays. *Phone:* (785) 472-5733. *Website:* myellsworth.com/echs/.

The site of the **first Fort Hays** (Fort Fletcher) is not marked but is visible from the road. To view, take Exit 172 off of I-70 at the village of Walker. Drive four and a half miles south on gravel road until you reach the historic Fort Fletcher (Walker) Bridge. The farm to your right before reaching the bridge is the unmarked site of Fort Fletcher.

Fort Zarah disappeared not long after its closing in 1869 as local settlers helped themselves to the building materials of the fort's structure. The post is commemorated by a roadside park three miles east of Great Bend,

Kansas, on U.S. Highway 56. Historical markers tell a bit of the fort's story, but the county museum south of Great Bend does have a small display about Fort Zarah. *Address:* Barton County Historical Museum, 85 South Highway 281, Great Bend, Kansas 67530. *Hours:* Summer (April to October), Tuesday through Friday, 10 A.M. to 5 P.M.; Saturday and Sunday, 1 to 5 P.M. Winter (November to March), Tuesday through Friday, 10 A.M. to 5 P.M. *Admission:* Non-members 16 and older $2. *Phone:* (620) 793-5125. *Website:* bartoncountymuseum.org.

After its closing in 1878, Fort Larned was sold to settlers and changed hands several times before the Edward Frizell family bought the property in 1902. The Frizells farmed and raised livestock while preserving the fort buildings and using some of them as a tourist attraction. The National Park Service bought the land and buildings in 1966 to establish the **Fort Larned National Historic Site**. One of the best-preserved forts on the Great Plains, Fort Larned features eight restored buildings and a reconstructed blockhouse originally dismantled around 1900. A map and guide are available at the visitor center for self-guided tours, but park rangers and other interpreters offer the best guidance. It's a very easy walk around the fort, with much to see. *Address:* 1767 Kansas Highway 156, Larned, Kansas 67550 (six miles west of the town of Larned). *Hours:* Open daily, 8:30 A.M. to 4:30 P.M.

The Fort Harker Guardhouse Museum includes a stone supposedly inscribed by Cody in 1874.

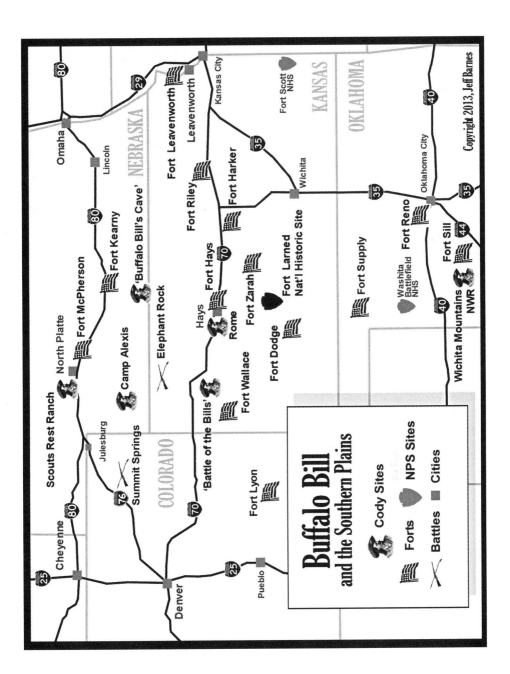

Buffalo Bill
and the Southern Plains

Cody Sites

NPS Sites

Forts

Cities

Battles

Copyright 2013, Jeff Barnes

The restored buildings of Fort Larned National Historic Site. The post stands as one of the best preserved on the Great Plains.

Closed Thanksgiving, Christmas, and New Year's Day. *Admission:* Free. *Phone:* (620) 285-6911. *Website:* www.nps.gov/fols.

Fort Dodge was closed and abandoned by the army in 1882, with the last of the troops assigned to Fort Supply in Indian Territory. In 1890 the old post became a state soldiers' home for veterans from the Mexican, Civil, and Indian wars, later joined by Confederate and black veterans, veterans from the Spanish-American War, Boxer Rebellion, both world wars, and the Korean and Vietnam wars. Today's Kansas Soldiers' Home is a modern long-term nursing facility within and among the fort's historic buildings, including the Fort Dodge Library and Museum (218 Pershing Street). The small museum gives the history of the fort through artifacts and displays. *Address:* 101 Pershing Street, Fort Dodge, Kansas 67843 (five miles east of Dodge City on Kansas 400). *Admission:* Free. *Hours:* Monday through Friday, 10 A.M. to 4 P.M. *Phone:* (620) 227-2121. *Website:* www.kcva.org/sh/.

Fort Wallace closed in 1882, and what nature and time hadn't diminished, area settlers soon did by hauling away buildings and their materials. The **Fort Wallace Cemetery** gave up its soldier burials to Fort Leavenworth when the post closed, although an **1867 cenotaph** erected by the men of the Seventh Cavalry and the Third Infantry remains. At the eastern edge of town is the **Fort Wallace Memorial Museum** with several displays on the post, including a diorama and many artifacts found on the fort site. *Hours:* Open from the first Monday after the first Sunday in May through October 1. Monday to Saturday, 9 A.M. to 5 P.M.; Sunday, 1 to 5 P.M. *Admission:* Free. *Phone:* (785) 891-3564. (For winter or after-hours visits, call 785-891-3780.) *Website:* www.ftwallace.com.

Not to be confused with the first Fort Lyon twenty miles to the east, the **Fort Lyon** visited by Buffalo Bill and the Fifth Cavalry avoided much of the Indian wars. Its most famous occupant was the great scout and army officer Kit Carson, who came here to die in 1868. Carson was later buried in Taos, New Mexico, and the home in which he died was reconstructed as a memorial chapel, which still stands. The post was closed in 1889 and reopened as a naval hospital in 1906 (the dry climate was thought helpful in treating sailors and marines suffering from tuberculosis). The Veterans Administration closed the hospital in 2001 and turned it over to the state, which operated it as a minimum-security prison through 2012. Now closed, the historic fort east of Las Animas on U.S. 50 sits vacant while the state and county wrestle over its future. During its use as a prison, access to the grounds to view the historic buildings was not permitted; at press time, the status of access was not known. The Kit Carson Memorial Chapel is a short distance within the gate. The Fort Lyon National Cemetery is also here, although the original fort burials were transferred in 1889 to Fort McPherson (Nebraska) National Cemetery when Fort Lyon was abandoned.

The **Skirmish at Elephant Rock** is about a mile south of Traer, Kansas, across Beaver Creek and north of a ridge containing Elephant Rock, a natural arch named for its resemblance to the large animal and its trunk. Unfortunately, the "head" section collapsed recently and the arch is no longer present.

The Kit Carson Memorial Chapel at Fort Lyon was constructed from the scout's original home. Cody would later name his son for Carson.

Related Site

Gen. Philip Sheridan envisioned a campaign of converging columns into the Indian Territory in November 1868. Cody was part of Carr's Fifth Cavalry, which was delayed by winter conditions; the Third Cavalry was halted for similar reasons at Fort Bascom in New Mexico. George Custer and the Seventh Cavalry did make it through, attacking Black Kettle's village of Cheyenne on the Washita River. Although controversial—for both the attack on a peaceful village and for Custer's abandonment of a missing officer and troops—the battle was the first victory for the U.S. Army in the Southern Plains campaign.

The National Park Service today operates the grounds as the **Washita Battlefield National Historic Site**, with a visitor center and trails on the battlefield. There are ranger-led tours on weekends, Memorial Day to Labor Day. *Address:* P.O. Box 890, Cheyenne, Oklahoma 73628. *Hours:* Visitor center open daily, 8 A.M. to 5 P.M., except Thanksgiving, Christmas, and New Year's Day. Overlook and trail open daily from dawn to dusk. *Admission:* Free. *Phone:* (580) 497-2742. *Website:* www.nps.gov/waba.

Bill and the Buffalo

Cody with his rifle, "Lucretia Borgia," and three unidentified men, circa late 1860s.

It's not known exactly when Bill shot his first buffalo, but it was likely in Nebraska along the Platte River during one of his boyhood trips out west with the shipping trains. There's also the legendary tale of his shooting a buffalo about to trample a small girl when he was with the Pony Express.

Cody's buffalo hunting began in earnest after a get-rich-quick effort in Kansas failed. He met a grader named William Rose, who proposed that Cody join him in starting a town to capitalize on the Kansas Pacific's coming through. Besides making money by selling lots, Cody may have wanted to follow in his father's footsteps as a town founder; whatever the reason, Cody agreed and the partners hired a surveyor to lay out a town about a mile northwest of Fort Hays. They named the town Rome, which within a month had around two hundred houses and three or four stores.

An agent for the railroad named William Webb proposed to Cody and Rose that he come in as a partner in the town. After they declined his offer, Webb laid out a new town that he called Hays City and announced that it would host the Kansas Pacific's shops and roundhouse. Within days the

This painting by Charles H. Stephens depicts Buffalo Bill's method of shooting buffalo by turning them into each other.

entire population of Rome moved to Hays City. Thus Cody was out of the town-founding business for almost the next thirty years.

Webb needed help, however, and hired Cody to work as a grader. One day a small herd of eleven buffalo appeared, and likely bored with the grading work, Bill cut loose the scraper from his horse, Brigham, jumped on (without saddle), and chased the beasts with the intention of taking a shot or two with his .50-caliber Springfield, nicknamed "Lucretia Borgia."

Before he got there, he ran into some officers from Fort Hays who were also chasing the buffalo. While they were simply following the animals, Cody said he anticipated where the buffalo would turn and rode off to intercept them, with Brigham instinctively closing in on the first.

"Raising 'Lucretia Borgia' to my shoulder I fired, and killed the animal at the first shot," he said. "My horse then carried me alongside the next one, not ten feet away, and I dropped him at the next fire." Before long, Cody said, he had killed all eleven with twelve shots. He claimed this was no great feat, but the officers were impressed. When the grading contract was completed, he took on a job in October as a hunter to supply meat to the workers building the Kansas Pacific Railroad. For twelve buffalo a day, he was paid five hundred dollars a month—considerable pay for the formidable dangers of hunting in Indian territory.

Cody wrote that during an eighteen-month period, he killed 4,280 buffalo for the work crews. As Don Russell points out in his biography of Cody, the time and the math don't add up. That eighteen-month stint overlaps with Cody's known activities elsewhere, and at twelve buffalo a day, he would have to have killed 6,570 buffalo. Russell considers it likely that a typographical error changed "eight months" to "eighteen months," but even within the shorter time period, the 4,280 buffalo claimed by Cody far exceeds the number which he was contracted to bag. If, however, he averaged twelve a day over a twelve-month period (from June 1867 to May 1868), he would be very close to his claim. In any event, he was killing many buffalo and earning a name for it.

According to Cody, the officers from Fort Hays took to calling him "Buffalo Bill" with the delivery of the daily rations. The nickname caught on, appearing in his hometown paper—perhaps in print for the first time—when the *Leavenworth Daily Conservative* wrote on November 26, 1867, of "Captain Graham . . . Buffalo Bill and other scouts." While at Fort Hays in August 1868, Major Armes wrote that "Bill Cody (Buffalo Bill), one of our scouts and one of the best shots on the plains, keeps us well supplied with plenty of buffalo and deer . . . and is one of the most contented and happy men I ever met."

Because buffalo and the name William were so common—and because the Great Plains was so vast—several men received the nickname "Buffalo

The First "Buffalo Bill"

There was one man who had a claim to being the first with the moniker "Buffalo Bill"—William E. Mathewson of Kansas. Sixteen years older than Cody, Mathewson came to the Great Plains as a trapper with the Northwestern Fur Company. In 1853, he established a trading post on the Santa Fe Trail, near today's Great Bend, Kansas.

In his day, Mathewson knew Kit Carson and the Kiowa chief Satanta, but the settlers of Kansas came to know him as the provider of buffalo meat to people starving after the harsh summer of 1860 and bitter winter of 1861–62. He shot buffalo daily out on the range for those who needed meat and earned the name "Buffalo Bill" because of it.

Mathewson was respected by the Indian tribes of his region and convinced their leaders to meet with government representatives for the Medicine Lodge Treaty in 1867. He was also instrumental in the release of fifty-four women and children held as Indian captives from 1868 to 1872.

William "Buffalo Bill" Mathewson.

Through his work in establishing the northern end of the Chisholm Trail, Mathewson became one of the founders of the city of Wichita. Working with the military in Kansas, he traveled to all of the forts and knew many of their officers, including George Armstrong Custer.

In 1911, Cody received a letter from a very irate Mathewson, telling him he had no right to call himself "Buffalo Bill," because he (Mathewson) was the original Buffalo Bill. "I aim to tell you to your face that you are using a title that doesn't belong to you," he concluded.

As history had already shown, the name was hardly owned by anyone until Cody made a spectacular career of it. Mathewson was probably correct that he was the original Buffalo Bill, but Cody wasn't about to share the name with anyone or have a public spat. He sent his press agent, Frank Winch, to meet with Mathewson at his home in Wichita, where Winch found out the old trapper had fallen on hard times and had to sell a rifle that he loved. The agent bought the rifle back and presented it in the name of Cody to "the original Buffalo Bill." The gesture touched Mathewson and the two met on excellent terms when Cody's Wild West came to Wichita. Cody even arranged to have Mathewson's life story told in weekly installments in a local newspaper (with Cody quietly paying for the stories).

Mathewson died at the age of eighty-six, five years after his letter to Cody. He is buried in Highland Cemetery in Wichita.

Bill": "Buffalo Bill" Cramer; "Buffalo Bill" Wilson; "Buffalo Billy" Brooks; W. C. Tomlins, the "Buffalo Bill of the Black Hills"; and, most prominently, "Buffalo Bill" Mathewson in Kansas.

There was also Billy Comstock, often called "Medicine Bill" but sometimes tagged as "Buffalo Bill." In early 1868, as the Kansas Pacific's construction steadily made its way west, a conflict erupted—or was created—between the hunters at Fort Hays and those at Fort Wallace over who could kill more buffalo. The officers at Hays backed Bill Cody; those at Wallace had their money on Comstock, who had been hired as a scout at Fort Wallace in 1866, and had served as chief scout for George Custer and the Seventh Cavalry during the 1867 campaign, but had returned to Fort Wallace by the fall of 1867.

The contest was advertised, and a special excursion train from St. Louis brought out around a hundred spectators, including Cody's wife and their daughter, Arta. The rules of the event were simple: the hunt would begin at 8 A.M. and end at 4 P.M., and both men would charge the same herd simultaneously. Referees would follow both to keep score. Whoever killed more would be declared the winner—and presumably have won the title of *the* Buffalo Bill.

When the men dashed into the herd, Cody said, it split. Comstock went left, and Cody went right. "My great forte in killing buffaloes from horseback was to get them circling by riding my horse at the head of the herd," Cody wrote, "shooting the leaders, thus crowding their followers to the left, till they would finally circle round and round." He fired fast and furiously and ultimately killed thirty-eight. Comstock, meanwhile, chased after the buffalo and fired at them from the rear, dispersing them over three miles and killing only twenty-three.

The hunters took a break for champagne with the spectators and then went back out—and again Cody killed more. Another herd, another chase— and Cody killed yet more buffalo. A break for lunch and more champagne followed, after which the game and outcome were repeated. For the final rounds Cody removed his saddle from Brigham and chased some of the buffalo toward the onlookers, dispatching them as they neared the crowd. The dust settled, and the final tally was

William "Medicine Bill" Comstock.

announced: Cody had sixty-nine, Comstock forty-six. The "true" Buffalo Bill was proclaimed, earned by deed and by witness.

Maybe.

The story of the "Battle of the Bills" is one of the more contradictory of the Cody legends. Some elements ring true, and others don't come close to being real. There's no record of the actual date of the hunting contest. No newspaper accounts have been found, nor letters or diaries from attendees. There are anecdotal accounts from people who were told of it, but no first-person accounts appeared until Cody's autobiography from 1879.

One element that doesn't ring true has to do with Comstock. Some months before the contest, he killed a contractor in an argument and went into hiding. At the time the contest is generally believed to have been held (spring or early summer of 1868), he was probably still on the lam. Comstock returned to scouting in August, presumably getting a reprieve when General Sheridan needed him, but it doesn't seem likely he would make himself visible before that time just for a bet.

Could the story have been fabricated? It's possible. Comstock was killed by Indians before 1868 was out and wouldn't have been around to dispute it a decade later. Without doubt, when promoters such as Ned Buntline started to build up Cody's legend for his stage career, it wouldn't do to have anyone to contradict the storylines.

Parts of the story do ring true, however. According to a scout and meat hunter at the time, the site of the contest was in a draw headed northwest from the railroad tracks, two and a half miles west of today's Monument, Kansas. Cody said it was twenty miles east of Sheridan, Kansas (near today's McAllaster), which also matches up. Years later, a Union Pacific section boss found several hundred beer and champagne bottles at the site, which indicates a very large party had taken place there. Why not a buffalo shoot?

The Trail Today

Although he did not maintain a permanent residence here, William F. Cody has strong ties to Hays, Kansas, and there are numerous sites that reflect that bond.

This obelisk marks the site of Rome, Kansas, William Cody's first effort at town-founding.

The restored officers quarters at Fort Hays State Historic Site.

The second Fort Hays has much more to offer as the **Fort Hays State Historic Site**. Operated by the Kansas Historical Society, the site and its spacious grounds contain four original buildings that have been restored or rehabilitated, including the 1867 limestone blockhouse, 1872 guardhouse, and two furnished officers' quarters out of the ten that originally occupied officers' row.

A newly refurbished visitor center and museum covers the role of Fort Hays in the Indian wars and displays a number of period firearms and Indian weapons. A touch screen explores the various fort buildings, a short video covers the Indian tribes in the area at the time of the fort, and there are life-like mannequins of Custer and Cheyenne chief Black Kettle. *Address:* 1472 Highway 183 Alt, Hays, Kansas 67601. *Hours:* Tuesday through Saturday, 9 A.M. to 5 P.M.; Sunday, 1 to 5 P.M.; closed Monday. *Admission:* Adults $3; seniors and students (K–12, college) $2; KSHS members, current military, and children 5 and under free. Annual passes available. *Phone:* (785) 625-6812. *Website:* www.kshs.org/places/forthays/.

After visiting Fort Hays, take the U.S. 183 bypass northwest and turn right (east) onto West Eighth Street/Old U.S. 40/North Campus Drive. You'll see a turn to the north in about a half mile—take this road north, across the Union Pacific tracks, to Twelfth Street, where you'll find a pyramidal limestone marker. This is the **town site of Rome**, the community founded by Cody in 1867. For eight months that year, this was the only town in Ellis County and the largest in western Kansas. Years after the Romans roamed across Big Creek to Hays, the marker was erected to commemorate the county's first town.

The marker doesn't tell the story of Rome, so for that and other fascinating tales of the area, drive into downtown Hays to visit the **Ellis County Historical Museum**. Located in not one but two former churches at the corner of Seventh and Main Streets, the museum presents the history of one of the wildest counties of the West, including one-time residents Buffalo Bill Cody, George Custer, and "Wild Bill" Hickok. It's a wonderful way to familiarize yourself with Hays. The museum also has walking-tour maps to direct you to the many historic sites in the downtown area. *Address:* 100 West Seventh Street, Hays, Kansas, 67601. *Admission:* Adults $6, children (6–12) $2. *Hours:* Tuesday to Saturday, 9 A.M. to 6

The depression at the center of this photo is the unmarked site of the legendary buffalo shoot between Cody and Comstock. The view is from U.S. 40, looking east toward Monument, Kansas, two miles distant.

A sculpture of Buffalo Bill closing in on a buffalo, west of Oakley, Kansas.

P.M.; Sunday, 1 to 6 P.M. Closed Mondays and major holidays. *Phone:* (785) 628-2624. *Website:* www.elliscountyhistorical museum.org.

Part of a walking tour is found five blocks north on Main Street at the Hays Public Library, which features a large heroic bust of Buffalo Bill near the entrance. This is one of many similar sculptures around the town.

The site of the contest with Comstock isn't marked, but it is easy to find and visible from the road. The draw lies half a mile west of U.S. 40's intersection with Kansas 25—as you drive west, the site is to the north of the Union Pacific bridge and tracks. A better view can be had from Day Dream Road, which runs parallel to the highway on the north.

A bigger "celebration" of the contest is found in Oakley, eight miles to the east of Monument. Traveling north on U.S. 83 (or four miles south from exit 70 on I-70), you'll soon see the **Buffalo Bill Cultural Center**, featuring a spectacular (twice life size) bronze sculpture diorama of Buffalo Bill chasing down one of the beasts. The event center has travel information and a gift shop. *Address:* 3083 U.S. Hwy 83, Oakley, Kansas 67748. *Cultural Center & Gift Shop Hours:* Monday through Friday, 10 A.M. to 5 P.M.; Saturday 11 A.M. to 5 P.M. *Phone:* (785) 671-1000. *Website:* www.buffalobilloakley.org.

A Home at Fort McPherson

Cody in the 1860s.

When Maj. Eugene Carr was transferred from the Department of the Missouri to Fort McPherson in the Department of the Platte, Carr was so impressed with Cody that he was granted an unusual request—to allow the scout to accompany him to his new post. Also at Fort McPherson in June 1869 were the Pawnee Scouts, headed by Maj. Frank North and his brother Luther. They were already well-seasoned for action against their traditional enemies, the Sioux and Cheyenne.

A successful expedition and ongoing scouting needs led to some permanence for Bill at the fort, which was located two miles south of the Platte River at the mouth of the Cottonwood Canyon. Expecting that he'd be here for a while, and having already come to love the countryside, Cody sent for his family in the spring of 1870. The Cody family increased by one on November 26 of that year with the birth of a son, named Kit Carson Cody after a suggestion by Frank North. Cody's second daughter, Orra, was born at the fort on August 13, 1872.

The Codys were entitled to free housing on post since Bill was a civilian employee, but he instead built a small home with a picket fence, frame windows, and carpet. Louisa started a dressmaking business, adding more income to the household.

For the next two years, Cody participated in campaigns throughout the region, often through the Platte River Valley for the Union Pacific, but also in the areas of the Republican, the Dismal, the Niobrara, and the Loup Rivers in Nebraska. There was plenty of action with the Indians, the most famous being the Republican River campaign of 1869, which resulted in the Battle of Summit Springs (see next chapter). Cody participated in a number of smaller affairs, too. In September 1869 he and Major North were surprised by Indians while establishing a camp for a column near Prairie Dog Creek in Kansas, barely escaping save for the timely arrival of a cavalry company.

Sometimes the range was much farther. In late May 1872, Cody and a cavalry detachment went in pursuit of a band of marauding Indians. They trailed the Indians to Fort Sully on the Missouri in the Dakota Territory before returning, stopping at Fort Randall on the southern end of the territory to resupply and rest the horses. When they got back to Fort McPherson on July 27, they had covered nine hundred miles.

After warriors raided the fort for horses, Cody and a lieutenant were sent in pursuit. They chased them for two days, destroyed their camp, and brought back most of the stolen stock. The annals of the Fifth Cavalry reported that Cody managed to shoot each of the raiders, but he didn't mention this in his autobiography.

Fort McPherson in the late 1860s at the time Cody lived at the post. NATIONAL ARCHIVES

Cody also had time for other pursuits. He acted as a guide for buffalo hunts out of the fort, engaged in horse racing for bets (apparently with success), and served as a justice of the peace at Fort McPherson, a task that required an army-connected civilian to mete out the law within the military reservation. A frequently told tale has Cody performing a marriage ceremony, during which, unable to find the official words, he supposedly substituted "whomsoever God and Buffalo Bill have joined together, let no man put asunder."

While at the fort, Cody was nominated in 1872 for a seat in the Nebraska legislature. He claimed he won the election but respectfully declined to accept because of pending show business offers in the East. The record shows that he actually wasn't elected but perhaps saw some early returns showing him in the lead. That was good enough for Cody, who wrote in his autobiography, "That is the way in which I acquired my title of Honorable"— which he frequently used in the early days of his show-business career.

After a time back east for his new career in show business, Cody worked out of Fort McPherson from August to October 1874, scouting for Capt. Anson Mills during the Big Horn Expedition. No Indians were found for

fighting during the expedition, but they did come across a former Custer scout, Moses "California Joe" Milner, who had been prospecting in the area. He tagged along with the column for a few days until he was hired on as a scout. The

Cody as justice of the peace at Fort McPherson, as depicted in his first autobiography.

Cody's Medal of Honor

A company of the Third Cavalry, guided by Cody, chased some Miniconjou Sioux after they stole horses from a Union Pacific depot near Fort McPherson. Cody found them in the treeless plains on the South Fork of the Loup River, on April 26, 1872, near today's Stapleton, Nebraska.

He, a sergeant, and ten men covered the south bank of the fork, while the rest of the troopers went to the north. Cody and his party found the Indians and charged them. Cody killed one man and the troopers two others.

The company commander, Capt. Charles Meinhold, said Cody guided the group "with such skill that he approached the Indian Camp within fifty yards before he was noticed. . . . Mr. William Cody's reputation for bravery and skill as a guide is so well established that I need not say anything else but how he acted in his usual manner." Meinhold submitted the names of Cody and three of the enlisted men for Congressional Medals of Honor. General Sheridan approved all of them, as did civilian officials.

By comparison with the stringent criteria required for the Medal of Honor today, the efforts of Cody that day seem minor, especially compared to other battles in which he fought. In 1872, however, this was the only medal offered by the Army. Valor wasn't the only criterion, either, and hundreds were awarded

for much less. One of the troopers with Cody was awarded the medal simply for following orders promptly and cheerfully.

Recipients weren't recognized at the White House as is today's custom; instead, medals were delivered through the mail. There were also plenty of phony medals and phony claimants out there, which was possibly why Cody rarely mentioned the honor.

The two Medals of Honor inscribed to Cody, as displayed at the Buffalo Bill Center of the West at Cody, Wyoming (left), and the Buffalo Bill Museum at Golden, Colorado (right).

The South Fork of the Loup River, site of Cody's Medal-of-Honor fight, looking east toward Stapleton, Nebraska, two miles away on the horizon.

The Army tightened the criteria for the Medal of Honor in years to come and began to review previous recipients. In 1917, one month after Cody's death, the medal was one of more than nine hundred rescinded because of his being a civilian scout when it was awarded. It wasn't until 1989 that the recognition was restored, with the Army Board for Correction of Military Records overriding the 1917 decision. The Medal of Honor stayed with the Cody family and Johnny Baker, Cody's foster son, after it was rescinded and is on display at the Buffalo Bill Museum and Grave on Lookout Mountain near Golden, Colorado.

There is also a Medal of Honor displayed at the Buffalo Bill Center of the West in Cody, Wyoming. It's virtually identical to the medal in Colorado, except for a shorter ribbon and a different inscription. The Wyoming medal (which was purchased from a collector) reads: "The Congress to William F. Cody Guide for GALLANTRY at Platte River, Nebr. April 26, 1872"; the Colorado medal reads "The Congress to William F. Cody Guide."

The specificity of the deed and location (even though it's the wrong river named) leads some to say that the Wyoming medal is the original. However, there is also an 1888 promotional lithograph showing the medal, with text that is closer to the Colorado medal's inscription, and a 1910 photo of Cody wearing the Colorado medal. One theory to account for two medals is that Cody gave the original medal away in the 1870s, later regretted it, and used his influence to have another made. Which is the original? It likely will never be known.

The unmarked site of the 1872 fight on the South Fork of the Loup River is visible to the north and west of the town of Stapleton, running parallel to Nebraska Highway 92; Stapleton is thirty miles north of North Platte on U.S. 83.

expedition was also known for nearly being trapped in the mountains by a freak snowstorm and for a trooper being killed by a bear.

The Trail Today

It's easy to forget that the vast majority of frontier forts were never meant to be permanent installations. Even so, one can be wistful for the great Fort McPherson at Cottonwood Canyon and the cedar-spotted hills south of the Platte.

The post was abandoned in 1880, but **Fort McPherson National Cemetery** remained. The U.S. government designated it a national cemetery in 1873, and as other forts in the region closed, their cemeteries gave up their dead to Fort McPherson. In fact, the soldiers of twenty-three posts are buried here—among them the enlisted men killed in the Grattan Massacre, the fight that began the Great Sioux War in 1854. Their mass grave and large white marble monument were originally at Fort Laramie, while Lieutenant Grattan himself went to Fort Leavenworth National Cemetery.

Fort McPherson National Cemetery also contains some of Buffalo Bill's scouting contemporaries, including the aforementioned Moses "California Joe" Milner, Baptistie "Little Bat" Garnier, and Spotted Horse, a Pawnee scout—all originally buried at Fort Robinson. (A mile south of the cemetery is a large stone monument commemorating the post and situated on the

Cody's fellow scouts Moses "California Joe" Milner and Baptistie "Little Bat" Garnier are among those interred at Fort McPherson National Cemetery.

Identified as the sole remaining structure from Fort McPherson, this log cabin is now at the Lincoln County Historical Museum in North Platte, Nebraska.

site of its flagpole. You'll see the sentry standing atop the marker.) *Address:* Fort McPherson National Cemetery, 12004 S Spur 56A, Maxwell, Nebraska 69151 (two miles south of the Maxwell exit on I-80). *Hours:* Office hours are Monday through Friday, 8 A.M. to 4:30 P.M. Closed federal holidays except Memorial Day. The grounds are open daily from dawn until dusk. *Phone:* (308) 582-4433 or (308) 582-4766 *Website:* www.cem.va.gov/nchp/ft mcpherson.htm#hi.

One structure from Fort McPherson survives today at the **Lincoln County Historical Museum**: the two-room log building identified as the fort's headquarters and a section of the fort's flagpole standing before the building. The museum itself contains numerous artifacts and displays from the county's rich history. *Address:* 2403 West Buffalo Bill Avenue, North Platte, Nebraska 69101. *Hours:* Monday through Saturday, 9 A.M. to 5 P.M.; Sunday, 1 to 5 P.M. (May through September). *Admission:* Adults (13 and up) $5, seniors $4, military (with I.D.) $4, children (12 and under) free, families $10. *Phone:* (308) 534-5640. *Website:* www.lincolncountymuseum.org.

Recommended Reading

Fort McPherson, Nebraska, Fort Cottonwood, N.T. by Louis A. Holmes (Lincoln, NE: Johnsen Publishing Company, 1963).

The Battle of Summit Springs

Summit Springs Rescue, 1869 *by Charles Schreyvogel (1908) portrays Cody in the heroic roll of shooting the Indian warrior who killed Susanna Alderdice.*

Almost immediately after arriving at Fort McPherson and requesting Cody in May 1869, Major Carr made preparations for patrolling the Republican River Valley, which passed through Colorado, Nebraska, and Kansas. This area was a favored hunting and camping region for the Cheyenne and Sioux, and they weren't going to leave it without a fight.

With Cody as their scout, Carr and the Fifth Cavalry left the fort on June 9 with orders to clear the Republican Valley of hostile Indians, including the Dog Soldiers of the Cheyenne. The undersized column of three hundred men had an additional one hundred and fifty Pawnee Scouts headed by Maj. Frank North of Nebraska. The column first moved to the south and then east along the Republican, followed by a swing down to the Solomon and back again to the Republican. An attempt by Cheyenne to raid one of the column's night camps was overwhelmed by the Pawnee, who killed two of the Cheyenne. Otherwise it was quiet.

Carr now moved west along the Republican in Nebraska. There was a small skirmish along Frenchman's Creek on July 6, followed by a second on July 8 at Dog Creek in Colorado. "I had little hope of overtaking the Indians," wrote Carr, "but thought I could at least hunt them out of the country." He pushed on for several days through the dry sand hills of eastern Colorado, headed for the South Platte River.

Cody told Carr that the Indians would need water and advised him to follow the faint trail they had found. At about two in the afternoon of July 11, Cody and some of the Pawnee Scouts found the village of Tall Bull's Dog Soldiers, with nearly eighty-five lodges and about four hundred people camped at a site called Summit Springs.

The column advanced as far as they could without being seen, and Carr then began the attack from the northwest. The buglers sounded the charge at about three in the afternoon. The cavalry caught the Cheyenne by complete surprise; most didn't even have time to catch their ponies.

As the troopers poured into the village, Indians attempted to kill two settler women captured in Kansas—Susanna Alderdice, who was brained by a tomahawk, and Maria Weichell, who was severely wounded. Tall Bull, the chief, along with

Tall Bull, as painted by H. H. Cross in 1867.
STATE HISTORICAL SOCIETY OF WISCONSIN

Gen. Eugene A. Carr.

some warriors, women, and children, took cover in a nearby ravine. The Pawnee Scouts played a major role in the attack in this area, and Cody killed Tall Bull very early in the fight. One of Tall Bull's wives and her daughter crawled from the ravine to surrender; a younger wife and another daughter had been killed.

Although most of the village escaped and the column was too exhausted to pursue, this represented a major victory for the Fifth Cavalry. In exchange for one man wounded, Carr reported the Fifth killed fifty-two Indians (not distinguishing by age and gender). More than four hundred horses were taken and the lodges and meat supply were destroyed. Seventeen women and children were captured, with most of the survivors fleeing Kansas to join the southern Cheyenne in Indian Territory. Except for a few minor incidents, the land between the Platte and the Arkansas had been cleared.

The Battle of Summit Springs was the archetypical Cody event, with incompatible stories that sometimes became wildly inflated.

For Cody's part, he claimed that he had earlier noticed Tall Bull riding an exceptionally fine horse. Intending to claim the horse for himself by killing its owner, Cody crawled as close as he dared to the ravine where the chief was hiding. When Tall Bull peered over the lip of the ravine, Cody took his shot from four hundred yards away (in later years he said it was thirty). The soldiers watching this were naturally impressed and later caught the horse to give to Cody as recognition for his skill and bravery. Cody went on to report that when Tall Bull's wife was captured several days later, she identified him—calling him *Pahaska* ("Long Hair")—as the one who killed her husband.

Although not at the scene, Carr wrote that Cody had killed the chief, as did other officers. Charles King, who joined the Fifth Cavalry as a first lieutenant two years after the fight (and later became a brigadier general), wrote that before 1929 he had never heard anyone doubt or question that Cody killed Tall Bull. Others who lived or served at Fort McPherson were documented as saying much the same.

Cody's wife said she read a newspaper account of the battle in St. Louis that reported Cody had saved Mrs. Weichell. When he returned home, she said, he laughed off the rescue, saying he didn't save her but did kill Tall

Frank North and the Pawnee Scouts

Frank North was a twenty-four-year-old clerk and interpreter at the Pawnee Agency when Gen. Samuel Curtis came to Columbus in Nebraska Territory in 1864. In the war against the Sioux, Cheyenne, and Arapaho that year, Curtis needed the help of the Pawnee, a traditional enemy of those tribes.

Although white, North was fluent in the Pawnee language from having lived and farmed near the tribe's reservation for the previous six years. Both his race and his language skills were immediate qualifiers to command a company of Pawnee; knowing him as a neighbor and a fair man was enough for the Pawnee to follow him.

In that year, and the years to come, the Pawnee Scouts were one of the most effective units for finding and attacking warring Indians on the Plains. North, promoted to captain, was quick to understand the fighting tactics of the Pawnee and exploit them against their enemies. Nearly every year until 1876, and always under Frank North, the Scouts organized in the early spring and mustered out in the late winter. They served in exemplary fashion at Fort Kearny, in the Powder River Country, and in protecting the transcontinental rail crews.

Maj. Frank North.

The scouts greatly admired Frank, whom they called "Grandfather" out of respect even though he was younger than many of them. After a fierce battle with the Cheyenne during the 1865 Powder River campaign, in which the scouts killed twenty-seven and took no losses or wounds themselves, they named him *Pawnee Leshar* or "Pawnee Chief."

They also thought he was invincible. During this campaign he became separated from his troops and was surprised by Sioux and Cheyenne. His horse was shot and injured, forcing North to use the steed as a walking breastwork while he fought off the Indians. He made it back to his men without a wound, confirming the Pawnee's belief that their commander had amazing powers.

By the time Buffalo Bill met up with the Pawnee Scouts at Fort McPherson, North was a major and his brother, Luther North, a captain of one of the Scouts' four companies.

(continued on page 74)

It wasn't long before Cody knew the value of the Indian allies. While on a scouting trip with Luther North and his men, he noticed one of the Scouts studying a field of grass. He asked North if the Pawnee had found a trail; North thought he had, but neither of them could see evidence of it. North told the scout that Cody doubted there was a trail, but the Pawnee pointed to a gap among some hills—three miles later at the gap, a clear trail of many Indian ponies was found.

"Well, I take off my hat to him," Cody was to have said. "He is the best I ever saw."

Frank North was post guide and interpreter at Fort D. A. Russell and Sidney Barracks (later Fort Sidney) from 1871 to 1876. After Custer's defeat at the Little Bighorn, General Sheridan ordered him to organize a company of Pawnee Scouts to join Gen. George Crook in his campaign of 1876–77. They assisted in the capture of Red Cloud and the engagement against Dull Knife before the command was mustered out in spring of 1877.

Cody was closer to Frank North than to Luther. Cody and Frank bought a ranch together on the Dismal River of Nebraska in 1877, and when they sold it in 1882, Frank joined Cody's Wild West the next year as a featured performer.

He was severely injured in 1884 in a riding accident during the show in Hartford, Connecticut, and was left in a hotel when the performing company had to leave for the next town. The Pawnee performers refused to leave North, certain he was going to die. It took tremendous persuasion from their "Grandfather," who had seven broken ribs and internal injuries, to convince them he wouldn't die. He had never lied to the Pawnee before, they said, and they left assured he would live.

The injuries left him in a weakened state, however, and he became seriously ill the next season while in New Orleans. He was transferred to Omaha, where Luther picked him up to bring him home to Columbus. Frank North died on March 14, 1885, at the age of forty-five. He was buried in the Columbus Cemetery and later joined by Luther, who died in 1935.

Bull. Confusing the situation even more, an 1897 *New York Herald* article quoted Cody saying he had saved a woman about to be killed and a Lieutenant Hayes had killed Tall Bull with a pistol.

Luther North tells an entirely different story, however, naming his brother Frank as the killer of Tall Bull. Luther told an interviewer that Cody was miles from the scene and didn't claim to have killed Tall Bull until the writer and promoter Ned Buntline met him a few weeks later.

Pawnee Scouts photographed by William Henry Jackson, around 1868–1871: From right: Man-Who-Left-His-Enemy-Lying-in-the-Water, Night Chief, One-Who-Strikes-the-Chiefs-First, and Sky Chief; standing is Baptiste Bayhylle, also called The-Heavens-See-Him-as-a-Chief, a Pawnee-French interpreter. SMITHSONIAN INSTITUTION, NATIONAL ANTHROPOLOGICAL ARCHIVES

Recommended Reading

Two Great Scouts and Their Pawnee Battalion: The Experiences of Frank J. North and Luther H. North by George Bird Grinnell (Lincoln: University of Nebraska Press, 1973); *Luther North: Frontier Scout* by Jeff O'Donnell (Lincoln, NE: J & L Lee, 1995); *War Party in Blue: Pawnee Scouts in the U.S. Army* by Mark Van de Logt (Norman: University of Oklahoma Press, 2010).

The Cody claim is somewhat diminished by Gen. Christopher C. Augur, commander of the Department of the Platte, who didn't mention Cody or the killing in the battle's official announcement. A joint resolution by the 1870 Nebraska legislature thanked Carr and Frank North for their services at the battle but said nothing about Cody—although the recognition could have been meant only for the leaders of the two major fighting groups.

Neither Cody nor Luther North remained consistent in their retellings of who killed Tall Bull. Both changed details of their respective stories enough over the following years that even proponents couldn't say which was true. And it's entirely possible—maybe probable—that someone else finished Tall Bull.

But it was definitely a "Buffalo Bill" story in the years to come, in both dime novels and in his stage performances. The story hit at just the right time for those fascinated by the disappearing frontier and for those who lived it. Summit Springs was the biggest battle of the campaign that year, but it's doubtful how well it would be remembered today if not for its promotion by William Cody.

The Trail Today

The **Summit Springs site** isn't difficult to reach, but it is on private land, which must be respected. Problems with those who have abused the site's access have brought some restrictions. From Exit 115 on I-76, drive south on Highway 63 for about five miles until reaching the Logan/Washington county line. Turn east on CR2/CR60 for four miles until arriving at the

A 1970 memorial to a Cheyenne herd boy is the most prominent marker at the Summit Springs battlefield that lies in the background.

forced left turn—you'll notice the signs indicating the private road and the direction to the Summit Springs site. This road is chained off—to see the site with its historical markers, you'll have to hike about three-quarters of a mile.

There are five markers at the site, the largest of which is a 1970 memorial to the fifteen-year-old Cheyenne herd boy killed while stampeding the village horses. There is also a 1966 state historical marker, a newer undated marker memorializing Susanna Alderdice (placed by author Jeff Broome), and two smaller markers for Tall Bull's lodge and Mrs. Alderdice's death site, both moved from their historic locations. The cattle pasture to the east is the battlefield and the ravine where Tall Bull was shot is visible to the right. No hiking is permitted beyond the fence surrounding the markers. There is also a 1934 state historical marker about two-and-a-half miles north of Exit 115, toward the village of Atwood, on the west side of Highway 63 just before reaching the South Platte River bridge.

Recommended Reading

The Cheyenne Wars Atlas by Charles D. Collins Jr. (Fort Leavenworth: Combat Studies Institute Press, 2010); *The Fighting Cheyennes* by George Bird Grinnell (Norman: University of Oklahoma Press, 1983).

Cody and the Great Buffalo Hunts

*Cody at Fort McPherson with some of his
hunting trophies and firearms, 1871.*

Scouting was not a preoccupation for Cody at Fort McPherson. "Although I was still chief of scouts," he wrote, "I did not have much to do, as the Indians were comparatively quiet, thus giving me plenty of time for sporting."

Cody was already out hunting for buffalo, antelope, elk, and other game to add to the officers' and soldiers' diet. Game was still plentiful around the fort in the late 1860s and early 1870s, and posts were encouraged to "live off the land" as much as possible. But hunting was also great sport for the officers and hunting enthusiasts like Phil Sheridan, who several times used Fort McPherson as his base of operations for great hunts with Cody as his guide. Sometimes Sheridan would refer friends and VIPs to Cody.

Cody was a natural for guiding hunters, with a lifetime love of hunting extravaganzas. He wrote in 1894 of being impressed by the English nobleman Sir George Gore, who came to Leavenworth in 1853 when Cody was but a boy. Gore paid for his hunting excursion himself and hunted alone, but hired about two hundred trappers and guides out of Fort Laramie. "He went in for genuine sport, and bade good-by to civilization when he left St. Louis," Bill wrote. "Buffalo, elk, mountain sheep, bear, and mountain lions were plentiful. . . . [H]e should, in these degenerate days, excite the wonder, if not the envy, of huntsmen who might vainly seek such glorious quarry anywhere in the great Rocky mountain region." When Indians attacked and ran off his horses at one camp, Gore and his men were forced to walk one hundred and fifty miles back to Fort Laramie.

In the winter of 1870–71, Cody met and guided Sir John Watts Garland, another great English huntsman he admired. Garland established a series of camps and cabins throughout the plains and mountains that he staffed with men to tend to his horses and dogs, to be readied when he returned to hunt every two years. "It was Sir John Watts Garland who, it seemed to me, first realized the value of the trained horse for hunting the buffalo," Cody wrote.

Cody's third "great hunter" was Windham Thomas Wyndham-Quin, the Earl of Dunraven. The earl came to Cody at Fort McPherson in 1869 bearing a letter of introduction from General Sheridan for Cody's guide services. Camping along

The Earl of Dunraven.

the Dismal and Loop Rivers in Nebraska, they hunted elk on horseback. It was no easy feat: faster than buffalo, the elk would allow them no closer than a half mile before running. "Then came the test of speed and endurance," wrote Cody. "[The elk] led the horses a wild race, and it put our chargers to their mettle to overtake the game. Right in among them we would spur, and, dropping the reins, use the repeating rifle with both hands."

The earl was a very wealthy man. He bought (some say stole) thousands of acres for a hunting park in Colorado that became the town of Estes Park. Cody said his first trip with Dunraven had them going out for four weeks, coming back to the fort to resupply, and then taking off again in another direction. An excursion for bear took them more than three hundred and fifty miles west of Fort McPherson to Fort Fred Steele on the North Platte River. Dunraven was the first of the visiting sportsmen to use a military escort on his hunts. "A lot of army wagons went along to take the game back to the fort, where it could be used," Cody wrote. "He was much opposed to any wanton waste."

A military escort was used in September 1871 for one of the largest hunts that Cody was to guide. This was the so-called "Millionaires' Hunt," hosted by General Sheridan for *New York Herald* editor James Gordon Bennett and around fifteen other industry tycoons, generals, and colonels, with about three hundred men accompanying them.

The hunt took the party south from Fort McPherson through the wooded Cottonwood Canyon for ten miles, where they emerged from high

ground to the Republican River Valley. From that point, they continued on into Kansas, past the Solomon and Saline Rivers, arriving at Fort Hays after ten days. This was a reversal of the route blazed by Custer four years earlier.

Cody's reputation was already well known before the men met him; now some positively adored him. "Tall and somewhat slight in figure, though possessed of great strength and iron endurance," Gen. Henry Eugene Davies wrote of their guide. "Straight and erect as an arrow, and with strikingly handsome features, he at once attracted to him all with whom he became acquainted."

Davies also noticed the stylish outfit Cody had for the hunt: light buckskin trimmed with buckskin

James Gordon Bennett, editor of the **New York Herald.**

Bird's-eye view of Fort Reno in 1891.

fringe, with a crimson shirt and broad sombrero. "Carrying his rifle lightly in his hand as his horse came toward us on an easy gallop," Davies wrote, "he realized to perfection the bold hunter and gallant sportsman of the plains."

Cody, a burgeoning showman, fit in very well with the show of this trip. Each night the camp was named for a member of the party ("Camp Cody" was established September 26 on Beaver Creek for the last night in Nebraska). Competitions were held, with trophies for the slayer of the first buffalo, first elk, first antelope, and so on. General Fitzhugh of Pittsburgh killed the first buffalo and won a silver drinking set embossed with buffalo heads. Their meals were prepared by French chefs and served by waiters in formal attire, on the finest china, linen, glass, and porcelain. For years to come, the campsites were commemorated by the many champagne bottles left behind.

There was plenty of hunting. An estimated six hundred buffalo were killed, along with two hundred elk and smaller game in proportion. The hunters left Fort Hays by rail, very happy with the ten-day hunt, and encouraged Cody to come to New York. He told them that would have to be cleared with Sheridan, who said, "By all means, yes—after the Grand Duke Alexis has had his hunt." This was the first Cody had heard of this upcoming hunt, which turned out to be perhaps the most famous big-game hunt in American history.

The last great hunt in which Cody wrote of participating—this time as a guest—was an 1892 hunt given by Gen. Nelson A. Miles, then commander of the Division of the Missouri. The hunt took them into the Indian Territory (now Oklahoma), where they started at Fort Supply. "I had my own tent, and military orderlies to come at my beck and call," Cody wrote, "and I soon got to imagine that I was Sir George Gore and the Grand-duke Alexis all rolled into one."

Buffalo Bill's Last Bison

Just as Custer had his Last Stand, Buffalo Bill had his "Last Buffalo." The only question is, where do you go to see it?

There are three contenders for the title of the last buffalo killed by William F. Cody, one in Colorado and two in Nebraska. Both have dates associated with them, and that should make it very clear which one is the last. But it doesn't.

The Buffalo Bill Museum in Golden has a mounted buffalo head in its exhibit. The information about the head reports that Buffalo Bill killed this, his last buffalo, in 1888, and that in 1915, he presented its mounted head to his friend with certification. The museum received the head in 1921.

The University of Nebraska State Museum, however, bought two stuffed buffalo from Cody in 1908, and they're still around today. One is at the university's Morrill Hall in Lincoln in a diorama with other buffalo. The second one is on display at the university's Trailside Museum at Fort Robinson State Park in northwest Nebraska.

A newspaper account from 1955 reported the buffalo at Morrill Hall was shot by Cody in the early 1900s in a canyon near North Platte, and the museum display states that it was the last buffalo killed by Cody; however, the museum also has a letter from Cody from 1912, in response to a query, stating that the buffalo were captured and raised near North Platte. What he didn't say in the letter was when the buffalo were captured, killed, and stuffed. Was it before or after the buffalo at the Colorado museum? If a "captive" buffalo doesn't qualify

Ben Clark.

From Fort Supply the hunt took them down the Canadian rivers to Fort Reno, then to the Washita River and into the Wichita Mountains. During the three-week hunt, Miles inspected the forts along the route (including Fort Sill among those previously mentioned) and held councils with the Indian tribes of the territory.

Cody said Miles took great delight in calling in old-time scouts and guides and having them join the hunt. Among them were Ben Clark, then the post scout and guide for Fort Reno, and Jack

One of two buffalo sold by Cody to the state of Nebraska. This one is located at Fort Robinson.

for the last buffalo killed, do we know whether the 1888 buffalo wasn't culled from the Wild West show? Does it matter?

In the end, Cody's "last buffalo" just wouldn't be part of his legend without some uncertainty to it.

Stilwell, who won fame by carrying dispatches to Fort Wallace through attacking Indians at the Battle of Beecher's Island.

Sadly, though, this was not a big-game hunt for Cody. The buffalo, elk, and antelope were long gone from that part of the territory, and only turkey, geese, prairie chickens, and deer were to be found.

The Trail Today

Much of the terrain is still the same as in Cody's day. Several of the sites visited by Cody in his hunting excursions still stand or are marked today.

He came to Fort Steele with the Earl of Dunraven; the fort today is **Fort Fred Steele State Historic Site**, ten miles east of Rawlins, Wyoming, on Interstate 80, Exit 228. The site, one mile north of the exit, is but a trace of what was once the fort; very few buildings still stand, and where foundations remain, many have caved in. This is also a very arid spot, despite

This sandstone marker, approximately eight miles south of Fort McPherson National Cemetery on Cottonwood Canyon Road, commemorates the trail taken by Cody and his hunting party in 1871.

being adjacent to the North Platte River. The state has invested in quite a few interpretive markers to tell Fort Steele's story, though, including its second life as the town of Fort Steele.

Other than the sites of Fort McPherson and Fort Hays book-ending the "Millionaires' Hunt," the only man-made marker alluding to the hunt is found seven miles south of the Nebraska fort. Here, in a field off of Cottonwood Canyon Road, is a sandstone marker to commemorate the **Fort McPherson Trail**. Listing the names of Cody, Sheridan, Custer, and other generals and scouts, the marker was erected in 1931. It's not known if it marks one of the hunt's campsites.

In Fort Supply, Oklahoma—the starting point of Cody's 1892 hunt with Nelson Miles—is the **Fort Supply Historic Site**, operated by the Oklahoma Historical Society. The five buildings that remain from the fort were there at the time of the Cody visit, including the 1892 guardhouse. That building is the museum for the site today, with artifacts and photographs from the fort. The site is located on the east entrance to the town of Fort Supply, alongside Highway 183. *Hours:* Tuesday through Saturday, 9 A.M. to 4 P.M. Closed on Sundays and Mondays (when the grounds are occupied by inmates of the adjacent minimum-security prison). *Admission:* Free. *Phone:* (580) 766-3767. *Website:* www.okhistory.org/outreach/military/fortsupply.html.

The 1892 guardhouse of Fort Supply, built in the same year as Cody's visit to the post.

Dominating the Fort Reno parade grounds during Cody's visit and today is the 1885–86 post commissary.

On the western outskirts of Oklahoma City (I-40, Exit 119), there are twenty-five buildings of **Historic Fort Reno** still standing after the post's closing in 1908 and subsequent repurposing as a remount depot, German POW camp, and agricultural research station. Highlights include a newly restored officers' quarters and visitors center, a chapel built by the POWs, and the imposing redbrick commissary. The post cemetery stands on a rise a quarter of a mile to the west; probably the most famous burial is that of the old scout Ben Clark, the last caretaker of Fort Reno. He committed suicide following a stroke in 1914, voluntarily ending more than fifty years of service to the U.S. Army. You can find his grave to the right after entering the cemetery. *Address:* Fort Reno Visitors Center, 7107 West Cheyenne Street, El Reno, Oklahoma 73036. *Hours:* Open daily, 10 A.M. to 4 P.M. *Admission:* Free. *Phone:*

Oklahoma's Wichita Mountains continue to host bison today, but as a national wildlife refuge rather than as hunting grounds.

(405) 262-3987. *Email:* info@fortreno.org. *Website:* www.fortreno.org.

The better part of a day can be spent poring through the history at **Fort Sill**, just north of Lawton, Oklahoma. This is an active army base (home of the Field Artillery School), but its museums and historic cemeteries have enough to keep a sightseeing visitor active as well. The Fort Sill National Historic Landmark Museum is the largest in the U.S. Army, with twenty-six structures for exhibit and storage. The new U.S. Army Artillery Museum incorporates the story of artillery from 1775 to the present, with more than seventy guns and artillery pieces. Outside the museum complex are the Apache Cemetery, with the burials of Geronimo and other prominent Apache leaders, and the Fort Sill Cemetery, nicknamed the "Indian Arlington." Here, on Chiefs Knoll, are the graves of Quanah Parker, Satanta, Satank, Ten Bears, Big Bow, Kicking Bird, and others. Admission to Fort Sill and its grounds is free, but be prepared to show your driver's license and auto registration for admittance. *Address:* 437 Quanah Road, Fort Sill, Oklahoma 73503. *Admission:* Free. *Hours:* Tuesday through Saturday, 8:30 A.M. to 5 P.M. *Phone:* (580) 442-5123. *Website:* sill-www.army.mil/museum/.

Immediately to the west of Fort Sill are the Wichita Mountains. When Buffalo Bill came here on his hunt with General Miles, the buffalo were already hunted to extinction there. They've since been restored to their natural setting as part of the **Wichita Mountains National Wildlife Refuge**. The buffalo you see here are descendants of fifteen buffalo that came to the refuge in 1907 from the Bronx Zoo; Quanah Parker himself was there to greet them. Besides buffalo, the refuge's 59,000 acres host elk, deer, longhorns, and nearly fifty other mammal species, along with many reptiles, birds, fish, and plants. The hiking is fantastic among the granite outcroppings and hardwood trees of the Wichitas—you'll easily see what attracted Cody. *Address:* 32 Refuge Headquarters, Indiahoma, Oklahoma 73552. *Admission:* Free. *Hours:* Monday through Friday, 8 A.M. to 4:30 P.M. *Email:* wichitamountains@fws.gov. *Website:* www.fws.gov/southwest/refuges/oklahoma/wichitamountains/.

The Royal Buffalo Hunt of 1872

Cody at the time of the Royal Buffalo Hunt.

In the fall of 1871, the Grand Duke Alexei Alexandrovich, the third son of Czar Alexander II of Russia, visited America on a goodwill mission. Earlier, knowing of the upcoming trip, painter Albert Bierstadt had suggested a hunting excursion to the grand duke while visiting St. Petersburg. Alexis expressed his strong interest in a hunt, and Bierstadt passed the information along to the White House after his return to the states. President Grant directed General Sheridan at the Division of the Missouri headquarters in Chicago to carry out the excursion. Having been on a number of buffalo hunts already, including the "Millionaires' Hunt" just a few weeks earlier, Sheridan knew whom he needed on the hunt.

George Custer was contacted in Kentucky, where the general was assigned to locate horses for the army. Custer brought the experience of hunting with royalty and celebrities, and Sheridan likely felt that that a senior officer with a still-youthful zeal would be best to instruct the grand duke in buffalo hunting.

Bill Cody, of course, already knew that he'd be the guide on this hunt. From Fort McPherson, he'd also try to find a friendly Indian tribe willing to break winter camp and demonstrate their hunting tactics and other customs for Alexis. According to Cody's autobiography, getting the Indians took extreme caution. Cody said that because of the likelihood of being killed should he openly try to reach the chief, he was forced to sneak into the camp of Brule Sioux chief Spotted Tail under cover of night to personally extend the invitation to the hunt. This was probably an exaggeration—it's more likely he forwarded the invitation to the tribe's Indian agent or walked into the camp with the agent.

Detail from an 1888 Buffalo Bill promotional poster showing General Sheridan assigning Cody to guide the Grand Duke Alexis on the buffalo hunt.

Grand Duke Alexis.

Cody was also charged with finding the herds and selecting a site for the hunting camp. He found buffalo about fifty miles to the south of the railroad town of North Platte. He also selected a site with a nice table overlooking Red Willow Creek where soldiers from Fort McPherson cleared the ground of snow to erect the tents for sleeping and dining.

Sheridan, Custer, and other officers from division headquarters came to Omaha on January 11, 1872. Alexis arrived the next day, and after a tour of the frontier city and a reception by local officials and citizenry, they crossed Nebraska overnight in specially appointed rail cars. They arrived in North Platte at 7 A.M. on Saturday, January 13, and were met by Cody, who was introduced to Alexis. Accompanied by two companies of cavalry and two of infantry from the fort, Cody led a group of around five hundred out of the town.

They first stopped for lunch and a change of horses at Medicine Creek, about halfway to the hunting camp. They arrived at "Camp Alexis" around 5 P.M. The Second Cavalry's band greeted the party with a rendition of "Hail to the Chief" and the Russian and American national anthems.

There was some celebration with champagne that evening—so much so that some of the hunters, Sheridan included, begged off from the first hunt. Cody, however, was up early to find the herd so that he could guide the hunters later. He returned to the camp at about 10 A.M., reporting the herd about fifteen miles away.

This first day of hunting on January 14—which happened to be the grand duke's twenty-second birthday—was not the "official" Grand Hunt. Spotted Tail's Brule Sioux had not yet arrived, and his braves were to join them the next day.

In this detail from **The Start of the Grand Hunt,** *photographed by Edric Eaton, Cody probably was finding the buffalo for the day's hunt. George A. Custer is second from the right, Grand Duke Alexis is fourth from the right, and Philip Sheridan is likely at the far left.*

Cody brought the hunters to the buffalo and, as he wrote in his 1879 autobiography, showed Alexis how to hunt. He put the grand duke on his own horse—Buckskin Joe—since it was accustomed to closing in on buffalo. Cody said Alexis took many shots at a bull with his pistol and then with Cody's pistol, neither of which had effect. He then was loaned Cody's favorite rifle, "Lucretia Borgia," and rode to within ten feet of the animal. Cody told Alexis when to fire and the resulting shot brought down the bull.

All of this may have been a fabrication. Cody was in the headlines of the newspaper stories, but according to the *New York Herald*, which had a correspondent at the hunt, it wasn't Buffalo Bill who was "assigned the duty of the initiation of His Imperial Highness into the mysteries of buffalo hunting"—it was Custer.

The *Herald* reported that the Duke, Custer, and Cody started out of the camp together, attracting the attention and admiration of everyone, while "The Grand Duke availed himself of Custer's experience, asked many questions, and practiced running and shooting at imaginary buffaloes as he went." Bill guided the party "up and down and round ravines," but there's no account of Bill loaning his horse, his gun, or his advice to Alexis.

The *Herald* gives an almost comical description of the initial charge: "The Duke and Custer charged together, but what seemed singular to the hunters the buffalo did not run; they stood at bay, as if they had been expecting the imperial party, and as if to say 'Come on.'" Custer charged through the herd to scatter them and identified a large bull. Alexis fired a few pistol shots into the animal, which fled into a ravine. The two followed, and "another pop from the pistol and he fell, when a shot from a rifle finished him."

Egos being what they are, it's difficult to believe that an experienced buffalo hunter and senior military officer like Custer—who thrived on entertaining the rich and famous—would turn over a prized guest to a civilian scout like Cody. Custer never wrote of his hunt with the Grand Duke. In his *My Life on the Plains*, he somewhat apologized for not including his hunting stories for fear it would make the memoir too long. (Alexis wrote a book in 1873 called *A Hunting Expedition on the Plains*, which might explain who did what, but it's not known if copies exist today.)

As the first accounts were made by a reporter who was there (and considering that Cody and his publicists were always looking for a good story, real or imagined), it seems likely that Cody didn't instruct Alexis to the extent claimed. In an 1894 magazine article by Cody, the only involvement he reported with the grand duke was the loan of Buckskin Joe. In an article for another publication three years later, the only personal involvement Cody described was traveling to see Spotted Tail to ask him to participate.

Cody was photographed by Edric Eaton in his Omaha studios. It is believed that because Cody missed having his photo taken at Camp Alexis, he had it done in the studio as a souvenir for Grand Duke Alexis.

Another stretched yarn had Sheridan telling Cody to take the reins of the grand duke's carriage on the return to North Platte and ride it as he had in his stagecoach days. Alexis was reported to have been shaken and thrilled by the wild ride. There are no reports of this ride by the accompanying correspondents, who recorded the journey back to North Platte without such an incident. It's difficult to imagine that such an important international guest would be subjected to danger.

If Cody did all of the things described, the newspapers covering the event completely missed them—which seems unlikely since they were hungry for all details relating to the hunt and these stories would have been very well received. It's not known if these exaggerations were Cody's own or were written for him, but he could hardly be blamed if he wanted a little more visibility from the trip. He missed being in camp for the few photos that were taken, probably done while he was out searching for the herds. The one shot that *was* taken of him for the souvenir photos was in Omaha while he was forwarding the buffalo head and hides for taxidermy.

At the conclusion of the hunt, the party returned to North Platte on the sixteenth. They had a banquet on the train before the group—without Cody—continued on to Cheyenne and then to Denver. Cody later wrote that Alexis wore a coat of many kinds of Russian furs during the hunt; he would carry the coat on his horse for the grand duke while the latter was shooting, and aid him in getting it back on when done. During the final night together, a count with the grand duke's entourage tried to pay Cody

A granite marker commemorates Camp Alexis and the occupants at the site.

for his services. The renowned guide politely turned it away. The count then said "His Highness wishes you to accept this coat" and gave him the admired overcoat.

Alexis also asked General Sheridan who was the best jeweler in America. When he was told Tiffany in New York, the grand duke told the count to write to the jeweler and have a set of jewelry made for Cody, studded with diamonds and rubies in the form of buffalo heads. Originally made as a tiepin and cuff buttons, they were later modified to a pin and ring for his wife and daughters. They are now on display at the Buffalo Bill Center of the West in Cody, Wyoming.

The Trail Today

The Royal Buffalo Hunt of 1872 is still remembered today in Hayes County, Nebraska. At the entrance to Hayes Center (the county seat) is a large steel sign with a buffalo, reading "Last Great Buffalo Hunt—Camp Duke Alexis— Jan 1872." At the east side of the village is the county courthouse, and in the lobby is a sandstone marker commemorating the hunt; it used to stand at the Camp Alexis site (erected by D. F. Neiswanger, who also put up the marker south of Fort McPherson for the "Millionaires' Hunt").

The state of Nebraska has a marker to the Grand Duke Alexis approximately nine miles to the east and north of Hayes Center at the intersection of Avenue 370 and Road 740A, near Red Willow Creek. (Do *not* travel these roads after a rain, the author advises from personal experience.) The site of Camp Alexis is approximately half a mile to the north on private land. There is a granite historical marker on the site of the camp to commemorate the hunt and its participants, erected in 1988 to replace the marker now in the courthouse.

Recommended Reading

Custer, Cody, and Grand Duke Alexis: Historical Archaeology of the Royal Buffalo Hunt by Douglas D. Scott, et al. (Norman: University of Oklahoma Press, 2013).

A Taste
of Fame

*Cody in his scouting garb, which
he also used for the stage.*

hortly after returning to Fort McPherson from the Battle of Summit Springs, Cody had the occasion to meet Ned Buntline, a heavy-drinking dime novelist who was passing through the Platte Valley, ironically giving temperance lectures.

"Dime novels" were sensational, superficial publications that were quickly written and cheaply produced for the mass market and its voracious readers. Buntline (whose real name was Edward Z. C. Judson) was a master of the medium, supposedly writing hundreds during his lifetime. When he met Cody, he was already rumored to be the highest paid writer in America.

Buntline originally sought out Wild Bill Hickok, but when Hickok ran him off, he instead spent time with Cody. They rode between the fort and O'Fallon's Station, with the writer quizzing the scout carefully about his profession. After returning to New York, Buntline wrote and published a magazine serial called *Buffalo Bill, the King of Border Men*. The stories bore little resemblance to Cody's experiences—Buntline would even later claim he invented his nickname—and Cody came across in the series more as a sidekick to Wild Bill Hickok than as a leading character in his own right. But the popularity of this thrilling series put Cody on the path to fame and fortune. Eventually, more than 550 different dime novels would be written about Buffalo Bill, including some by Cody himself.

The result of this popular press was that imprint greatly increased numbers of VIPs to Fort McPherson wanting its chief of scouts to guide their hunting parties. After the Millionaires' Hunt of 1871 and the Royal Buffalo Hunt of 1872, Cody was ready to take a swim in the waters of celebrity.

Securing a leave of absence from scouting, Cody visited Chicago and New York to renew friendships he made on the 1871 hunt. *Buffalo Bill: The King of the Border Men*, a play based on Buntline's original dime novel, happened to be premiering in New York's Bowery Theatre. Cody had a reserved box and was announced by the actor playing him. "The audience, upon learning that the real 'Buffalo Bill' was present, gave several cheers between the acts," wrote Cody, "and I was

Ned Buntline.

The stars of Scouts of the Prairie *(from left): Ned Buntline, Cody, Giuseppina Morlacchi, and Jack Omohundro.*

called on to come on the stage and make a speech." In his first time before an audience, he said he fumbled at making a few words. It was nothing to be proud of, but he came across as authentic. The theater owner offered him $500 a week to join the production, but Cody declined.

He also met with Buntline, who interviewed Cody for material for a play of his own and more dime novels about the scout. The plainsman was certainly starting to realize, if he hadn't already, that there was the potential for substantial earnings just by "being" Buffalo Bill.

Cody returned to Nebraska for a summer of scouting, but Buntline continued to pester Bill to return to the East and the stage, promising far more than his scouting contract. After eight months, Cody relented and went to New York to "try my luck behind the footlights." He would be the star of a new play written by Buntline called *Scouts of the Prairie*, also featuring old scouting friend Texas Jack Omohundro, Italian ballerina Mademoiselle Giuseppina Morlacchi (who would later marry Omohundro), and Buntline.

The scouts had no acting experience—and it showed—but the audiences didn't care. They were thrilled to see Buffalo Bill and Texas Jack in person, and the show was a huge success in every town where it played. When *Scouts of the Prairie* came to St. Louis, Cody was able to spend time with Louisa and their three children, who had moved to the city when he left Fort McPherson.

Shortly after leaving St. Louis, Cody moved his family to Pennsylvania and then to Rochester, New York, in order to be closer to them in his new career. Problems were developing in their marriage with Cody on the road; Louisa was nagging incessantly, jealous of the women that flocked to his shows.

The first season of *Scouts of the Prairie* ended in June 1873. After Buntline took his generous cut of the receipts, Cody and Omohundro were disappointed to find they were only making $250 a week. They took their dissatisfaction back to Nebraska for the off-season and returned with plans to start their own acting company.

They talked their old pal Wild Bill Hickok into joining the company and hired publicist, show manager, and sometime-actor John M. Burke. The relationship between Buffalo Bill and Burke would continue through the rest of Cody's life.

Hickok didn't finish the season (see sidebar on pages 17–18). Omohundro and his wife left the show after a year but still performed from time to time. Cody and Burke created a new production troupe called the Buffalo Bill Combination, which performed a single play for the season and replaced it with a new one the next year. Cody continued to travel west in the spring on scouting duty for the Army, but now devoted autumn and winter to show business.

Louisa and the children often traveled with him on the theater circuit, leading to occasional exchanges during the show. At a performance in St. Louis, with Louisa's family in the audience, Cody was having a bad time with his lines when he saw her. "Oh, Mama, I'm a bad actor!" he called

An advertisement for **Scouts of the Prairie.**

Kit Carson Cody, Buffalo Bill's only son, died in 1876 of scarlet fever. After Louisa had the boy's hair curled into ringlets, Cody insisted on cutting them off. Louisa said the haircut resulted in a chill that led to his illness and death.

out, leading to cheers and acceptance from the audience.

Young Kit Carson Cody loved to watch his father perform and got to the theaters early to watch the crowds come in. As Bill came out on the stage, Kit would call out "Good house, Papa!" to the laughter of the audience and the pride of the father.

Cody spent the summer of 1875 in Rochester. That same year, he wrote his first dime novel. He added several more over the next ten years. Still others appeared under his name that were probably written for him by ghostwriters. His autobiography came out in 1879 with stories of varying degrees of truth and would be rewritten and republished many more times in his lifetime.

The Combination reunited that fall for another touring season. While in Massachusetts in April 1876, Cody received word that Kit was seriously ill with scarlet fever. He rushed home in time for "Kitty" to die in his arms. The loss was devastating to Cody, who loved all of his children but adored his only son. He would dote on his daughters from this point on and always welcomed children to his tent when he took his productions on the road.

The Trail Today

One of the Codys' Rochester homes still stands at 407 Frederick Douglass Street. The Cody House, as it is called today, is a sixteen-bed community residence that serves male adults in recovery from chemical dependency. There are no tours, and it is not open to the public. Another residence at 8–10 New York Street is gone and now a vacant lot.

Cody's son, Kit, is buried at the city's **Mount Hope Cemetery**, along with his daughters, Orra and Arta, who died in 1883 and 1904, respectively. (Tragically, Cody outlived all but one of his children.) Adjacent to the Cody children's gravesites is that of Johnny Baker, Cody's foster son. Baker established the museum on Lookout Mountain in Colorado, next to Bill's grave. When he died, his wish to be buried near the other Cody children was fulfilled.

Mount Hope is the city's oldest cemetery and the site of many notable graves, including abolitionist Frederick Douglass and suffragist Susan B. Anthony. This was also the burial site of Henry Ward, an "Indiana Jones"–type scientist and friend of Cody's; his business, Ward's Natural Science, collected fossils and other specimens from around the world to sell to colleges and museums. He was the first auto fatality—a hit-and-run victim—in Buffalo, New York; his ashes were stolen from his crypt at the cemetery and never recovered. A huge jasper-flecked boulder found by Ward serves as his memorial. *Address:* 1133 Mount Hope Avenue, Rochester, New York 14620.

Recommended Reading

The Lives and Legends of Buffalo Bill by Don Russell (Norman: University of Oklahoma Press, 1960); *Buffalo Bill's America: William Cody and the Wild West Show* by Louis S. Warren (New York: Knopf, 2005).

The Road to Warbonnet

*Cody in the distinctive outfit he wore at Warbonnet
and later in his stage portrayal of the fight.*

apt. Anson Mills of the Third Cavalry wrote letters in the spring of 1876 urging Cody to join Crook's summer Sioux War command. The death of his son and his theater obligations held him, but at Cody's final show of the season, he announced to his audience that he was done acting for now and off to fight in the Indian wars. Four days later, on June 9, 1876, Bill was in Cheyenne, Wyoming Territory.

Cody was met at the Union Pacific Depot by 1st Lt. Charles King, who took him to nearby Fort D. A. Russell. Eugene Carr, now a lieutenant colonel, and the Fifth Cavalry had returned to the plains from Arizona. Cody returned to his old regiment to the cheers of the camp.

The symbolism to the troopers of Cody and Carr reunited can't be underestimated. "All the boys in the regiment exchanged confidences and expressed themselves to the effect that with such a leader and scout they could get away with all the Sitting Bulls and Crazy Horses in the Sioux tribe," wrote an enlisted man.

The column was first ordered to Fort Laramie and service on the Cheyenne River, while Cody joined General Sheridan and went to Camp Robinson and the Red Cloud Agency in Nebraska. Unknown to any of the parties yet was Crook's failure at the Rosebud on June 17.

While at Camp Robinson, Lt. Col. Wesley Merritt was named on July 1 as colonel of the Fifth Cavalry, succeeding William Emory, who had been on detached service since 1871. Merritt was already at Robinson as an inspecting quartermaster, and when he rode to assume command of the Fifth, Cody accompanied him.[*]

Following a brief chase of some Indians found along their route, Merritt decided to rendezvous at the small army camp on Sage Creek, adjacent to the Hat Creek Station on the Cheyenne–Black Hills Road.

_____

[*] Carr was the lieutenant colonel and field commander of the Fifth, second in command to Merritt—much as Lt. Col. George Custer was field commander of the Seventh yet second to Col. Samuel Sturgis at regimental headquarters. Custer, Carr, and Merritt were all brevetted as generals during the Civil War and, per custom, were often called "general" following the war.

Lt. Col. Wesley Merritt.

The dramatic news from Little Bighorn finally reached the camp on July 7. As recalled by Lieutenant King, Cody approached him and his fellow junior officers after hurrying from Merritt's tent. "His handsome face wore a look of deep trouble," wrote King, "and he brought us to a halt in stunned, awe-stricken silence with the announcement, 'Custer and five companies of the Seventh wiped out of existence. It's no rumor—General Merritt's got the official dispatch.'"

The Fifth was ordered to join Crook on July 11 and headed toward Fort Laramie to prepare. One day away from the fort, however, Merritt received word that some eight hundred Northern Cheyenne were about to leave the Red Cloud Agency. He decided to backtrack the seven companies of the Fifth and intercept the Cheyenne on the trail.

Through a series of "lightning marches," they began a fifty-mile march on July 16 to the Sage Creek army camp. By 9 P.M., they were in Nebraska on Warbonnet Creek, ahead of the Cheyenne.

Cody found the Cheyenne camp the next morning and notified Merritt that they were preparing to move. He, Merritt, Carr, King, and a few other staff officers waited on a conical hill overlooking the trail and the Warbonnet Valley to await their coming. Indian scouts appeared at 5 A.M. on the seventeenth, moving slowly, hiding from Merritt's oncoming supply wagons to the west. When army couriers were spotted by the Cheyenne, they prepared to attack. Cody told Merritt he could cut them

Camp Robinson, renamed as Fort Robinson in 1878.

The Hat Creek Station, seen here in 1880, was established in 1875 by Capt. James Egan, who built the station to the north of the Hat Creek Breaks on Sage Creek. Some say he mistook the stream for Hat Creek in Nebraska; perhaps he named the station after the breaks. Since then, Sage Creek has become known as Hat Creek.

off and was allowed to lead two army scouts and five or six troopers to engage.

Buffalo Bill was remarkably visible that day, wearing a Mexican *vaquero* outfit of black velvet and scarlet, trimmed with silver buttons and lace. He knew there would be a fight, and he dressed for a role he could play on the stage. Perhaps he anticipated the news accounts and their descriptions of what he wore during this self-expected act of valor. Almost assuredly, he wanted to tell his audiences he was wearing the same scouting uniform on stage that he had worn that day. But it's also possible that was the only outfit he had available that day.

The terrain blocked the officers on the hill from seeing what happened next, but a shot was heard and then a second. A signalman, Christian Madsen of Company A, said he saw through his telescope that both the scouts and the Indians appeared surprised to meet each other. "Cody and the leading Indian appeared to be the only ones who did not become excited," he later wrote. "The instant they were face to face their guns fired. It seemed almost like one shot. . . . They met by accident and fired the moment they faced each other."

Madsen said Cody's shot passed through the Indian's leg and dropped his horse, while the Indian's shot went wild. Cody's horse apparently stumbled in a gopher dog hole, so he jumped clear of his mount, kneeled, and took a second shot almost simultaneously with the Indian's second. Cody's hit the Cheyenne in the head while the Indian's missed again. Madsen said Cody then took the Indian's scalp along with his war bonnet, shield, bridle,

"The first scalp for Custer," as depicted in Buffalo Bill Cody's 1879 autobiography.

whip, and weapons, while the rest of the troops chased the other mounted Indians. The Indian killed by Cody was later identified as a warrior named Yellow Hair, who has been frequently misnamed as Yellow Hand.

The "battle" mostly fell apart at this time. Two other Indians were reported killed, but the remaining warriors in the field and tribesmen behind returned to the agency that day. Merritt had about three hundred and fifty soldiers ready to fight twice as many Indians but said he never saw more than thirty. Carr, in telling his wife about the Warbonnet fight, later didn't find the affair worth much. "There were a few sacks of flour destroyed, three Indians killed, 12 ponies captured and a few went back to the Agency," he groused.

Crook was critical because the side trip to Nebraska had delayed the troops that he sorely needed after his defeat at the Rosebud. But Sheridan commended Merritt for the quick action to stop the Cheyenne. In fact, it was the first bright spot for the army in the unfolding Great Sioux War.

Cody wrote to Louisa from the Red Cloud Agency the next day that "We have had a fight. I killed Yellow Hand a Cheyenne Chief in a single-handed fight. You will no doubt hear of it through the papers." He mentioned that when he reached Fort Laramie, he would send the battle souvenirs to display in a Rochester shopkeeper's window.

Cody reenacted the scalping of Yellow Hair in a 1913 film series covering the events of his life.

Lieutenant King reported that the agency Indians "one and all wanted to see Buffalo Bill, and wherever he moved they followed him with awe-struck eyes." They didn't have long to look because the Fifth was back on the trail to Fort Laramie on the eighteenth.

Word of Buffalo Bill's "duel" with Yellow Hair evolved quickly. On stage and in a serialized novel, Cody depicted the Warbonnet skirmish as a much larger affair in which three Indians had already been killed before he and Yellow Hair met. The Cheyenne in this instance knew Cody and challenged him aloud to a fight. They charged each other and fired, with Cody now hitting him in the breast rather than leg. In this version, Cody moved swiftly upon the Indian with a knife that he buried in Yellow Hair's heart. "I scientifically scalped him in about five seconds," Cody wrote. "As the soldiers came up I swung the Indian chieftain's topknot and bonnet in the air and shouted: 'The first scalp for Custer.'" This version was repeated in Cody's autobiography three years later, making it part of "official" Buffalo Bill lore.

The book by Cody's sister, Helen Cody Wetmore, had its share of exaggeration. In her account, Yellow Hair rode back and forth before his warriors, taunting Cody to engage in a duel like a pair of jousters. As soon as Yellow Hair was killed, "some two hundred warriors dashed up to recover the chieftain's body and to avenge his death."

Nebraska author Mari Sandoz—no fan of Buffalo Bill—claimed that Yellow Hair taunted the troopers until one angered trooper fired and killed the Indian; that same trooper then scalped him. "Cody paid him five dollars

The 1934 dedication of the monument marking the site where Cody killed Yellow Hair. Johnny Baker initiated the marker but died before its completion; his widow, Olive (to the right of the marker), attended for him.

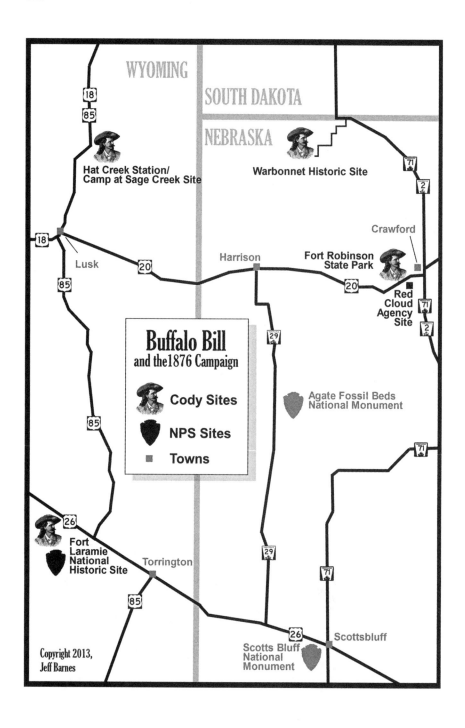

WYOMING

SOUTH DAKOTA

NEBRASKA

18

85

Hat Creek Station/
Camp at Sage Creek Site

Warbonnet Historic Site

71

2

Crawford

18

Lusk

20

Harrison

Fort Robinson
State Park

85

20

Red
Cloud
Agency
Site

71

2

85

Buffalo Bill
and the 1876 Campaign

Cody Sites

NPS Sites

Towns

29

Agate Fossil Beds
National Monument

85

71

26

Fort
Laramie
National
Historic Site

Torrington

29

71

85

29

26

Scottsbluff

Copyright 2013,
Jeff Barnes

Scotts Bluff
National
Monument

for the scalp that night," she wrote, "and it is presumed he came into possession of the warbonnet by similar means."

Like Custer's battle at the Little Bighorn, in which many claimed to be survivors, so too did others claim to have shot, saw someone else shoot, or even assisted, so Cody could get the shot against Yellow Hair. Most of these individuals were not at the skirmish, and the regimental history of the Fifth Cavalry makes it clear that Cody, "the favorite scout of the regiment, was conspicuous in the affair of the morning, having killed in hand-to-hand conflict, Yellow Hand, a prominent Cheyenne chief."

Also similar to the Little Bighorn battle, Buffalo Bill's "duel" at Warbonnet was destined to inspire artistry. This minor event in the Plains Indian wars would be considered the second-most important battle of all if based on the artwork it generated. The paintings, drawings, or sketches depicting the event number well into the hundreds, placing Yellow Hair among the pantheon of Indian subjects in art. Don Russell wrote that Yellow Hair was truly unique among all Indians, "for no other of his race ever died so often, in so many different places, by so many different hands."

Buffalo Bill Cody took part in fourteen fights against Indians, but it was his last that became the most famous, almost entirely as a result of his publicity efforts. If Cody had not been at the skirmish at Warbonnet, few would have heard of the fight.

The Trail Today

Cody's first stop with the Fifth Cavalry in Crook's Bighorn and Yellowstone campaign of 1876 was the nine-year-old post of **Fort D. A. Russell**, west of Cheyenne. The fort was a cavalry post until 1927 and was renamed Fort F. E. Warren in 1930; following World War II, the army air corps post was renamed again as F. E. Warren Air Force Base. This is an air base without a runway as Warren is the home of about one hundred and fifty Minuteman II missiles.

Among the more than two hundred historic buildings on the base is the 1894 post headquarters building that is today's **Warren ICBM and Heritage Museum**. The museum includes both the missile and cavalry history, with many artifacts filling the two floors of the building. *Address:* 7405 Marne Loop, Building 210, F. E. Warren AFB, Wyoming 82005. *Hours:* Monday through Friday, 8 A.M. to 4 P.M. Closed weekends and holidays. *Admission:* Free. (Identification and vehicle registration are required for access to the base.) *Phone:* (307) 773-3381. *Website:* www.warren.af.mil.

Fort Laramie was already one of the oldest forts on the plains when Cody and the Fifth Cavalry came through in 1876. Today's **Fort Laramie National Historic Site**, established in 1938, is one of the longest-operating

Cody and Custer: Friends or Foes?

William Cody took "the first scalp for Custer" in the fight at Warbonnet Creek. As presented in his Wild West, it was almost as if he was avenging the murder of a friend.

This impression was reinforced whenever Cody referred to the dead commander. In his first autobiography, Cody wrote of guiding Custer in 1867 from Fort Ellsworth to Fort Larned. According to Cody, Custer said he'd like Cody to accompany him as one of his scouts someday, Cody wrote, "and he added that whenever I was out of employment, if I would come to him he would find something for me to do. This was the beginning of my acquaintance with General Custer, whom I always admired as a man and as an officer."

Although Cody spoke highly of Custer whenever asked and referred to a strong relationship from that first meeting, it's likely they had little to do with each other. They probably saw each other when both were at Fort Hays in the late 1860s, but neither wrote of the other while there. Their only recorded meeting—outside of Cody's autobiography—was during the Royal Buffalo Hunt of 1872. Of the photos taken during the event, there are none with Custer and Cody together, and there are no accounts of the two interacting with each other.

They certainly knew of each other, because they were both in the business of guiding the rich and famous on buffalo hunts. Custer was well established as the Civil War's "boy general," as the country's premier Indian fighter, and as a published author of his hunting adventures. Cody's celebrity was just getting started through dime novels and as a favored guide and scout for the Army.

It's not difficult to imagine some jealousy between the two buckskinned "white Indians." In putting on hunting excursions, Cody probably coveted Custer's regimental band, supply wagons, packs of staghounds and deerhounds, and successful series of articles for sportsmen magazines.

But as Cody started to accumulate fame and fortune on the East Coast as a performer in the early 1870s, Custer probably felt *he* should be enjoying that life. He explored leaving the Army to go on the lecture circuit himself. Not a great speaker, Custer tended toward nervousness when he had the podium. But the promise of large audiences and a check to go with it was enticing. He wrote to his brother Tom in January 1876 that an agency in Boston was prepared to offer him a contract for $200 a night, five nights a week for at least a month. It was considerable money, but Custer turned them down, saying he needed more time to prepare. Instead of lecturing that spring, he and the Seventh went to Little Bighorn.

But Cody and Custer didn't "pal around," and they likely wouldn't have. As pointed out by Louis Warren, Cody would have avoided someone like Custer.

*Custer and the Grand Duke Alexis were pho-
tographed in St. Louis following their buffalo
hunt; years later, Cody was added to the shot.*

The general was a controversial figure
and not widely loved, even in his own
regiment. Cody, on the other hand,
enjoyed the company of nearly everyone
and the feelings were typically mutual.
He rarely took sides in a division and
avoided controversy.

Perhaps by avoiding Custer or being another favorite of Phil Sheridan,
Cody incurred Custer's scorn. It wasn't that Custer said anything "bad" about
Cody; he just didn't say anything at all. In his 1874 memoir, *My Life on the
Plains*, Custer wrote that Bill Comstock "was the favorite and best known scout
on the central plains . . . the superior of all men who were scouts by profession
with whom I had any experience." He told tales of Wild Bill Hickok, "then and
now the most famous scout on the plains," as well stories about scouts Moses
"California Joe" Milner and Ben Clark, but nothing about Buffalo Bill.

This was at the same time Cody was gaining fame onstage as one of
the great scouts of the plains and two years after he and Custer had hunted
together with the Grand Duke Alexis. Did Custer omit the scout from his book
because he was jealous of him? If Cody thought they had any kind of relationship, the slight had to have been crushing, but if they were private adversaries,
he couldn't have been surprised.

In spite of Custer ignoring him in his writing, Buffalo Bill heralded the
deceased Custer on the stage. Reenactments of Custer's Last Stand and the
Warbonnet fight were soon major presentations in his Combination shows and
his Wild West, drawing thousands of customers to see the spectacle and presumably creating Custer fans for years to come.

Cody, or at least his publicists, further attempted to improve his status
within the Custer legacy. The story of the contest between Comstock and
Cody, in which Cody bested Custer's favorite scout, appeared *after* Custer's
death. More colorful accounts of Buffalo Bill during the Royal Buffalo Hunt
started to appear. Even a photo of Custer and Alexis taken during the hunt
was doctored to add Cody to the shot.

There is a certain irony in the relationship between Custer and Cody. When
they were contemporaries, neither was inclined to do the other any favors;
however, when Custer was gone, Cody enhanced Custer's reputation along
with his own.

The former post headquarters of Fort D. A. Russell is today's Warren ICBM and Heritage Museum at Warren AFB.

Fort Laramie National Historic Site.

The Hat Creek Station that Cody saw in 1876 was replaced in the 1880s with this station.

historic properties within the National Park Service. It is also one of the best-preserved forts of the Great Plains. Nearly a dozen buildings were saved and restored to their original appearance, and nine standing ruins complete the structural landscape of the fort. The most featured of the existing buildings is the oldest—the bachelor officers' quarters, better known as "Old Bedlam," constructed in 1849. The site's visitor center hosts an orientation film and one of the best bookstores on the plains. *Address:* 965 Gray Rocks Road, Fort Laramie, Wyoming 82212. *Hours:* Museum and visitor center opens at 8 A.M. with varying hours of closing throughout the year. Fort grounds open from dawn to dusk daily. *Admission:* Seven-day pass, $3; annual pass, $15. *Phone:* (307) 837-2221. *Website:* www.nps.gov/fola/.

To reach **Hat Creek Station**, drive U.S. 85 north from Lusk for about thirteen and a half miles. Turn right (east) onto Hat Creek Road and drive two miles until you reach the old school house. Turn right (southwest) onto Stage Road and drive one mile. The large, two-story log structure on the right is the old Hat Creek Station. It was built in the 1880s after Cody's visit and is located on private property. The army **Camp at Sage Creek** essentially surrounded this site. The Hat Creek name is somewhat of a misnomer as the adjacent stream was originally called Sage Creek.

Returning to Lusk, a worthwhile stop is the **Stagecoach Museum** at 322 South Main Street, featuring much of the areas's nineteenth- and twentieth-century history. Most importantly, there is an authentic Black Hills stagecoach

Fort Robinson State Park in Nebraska's Pine Ridge.

The Warbonnet battlefield today. The hill in the background was the observation point for Cody, Merritt, and others; the fenced marker in the foreground is the site of Cody's killing of Yellow Hair.

in their collection. *Hours:* Open Monday through Saturday, 10 A.M. to 4:30 P.M., and by request on Sunday. *Admission:* Adults $2. *Phone:* (307) 334-3444. *Website:* niobraracountylibrary.org/museum/.

From Lusk, eastbound U.S. 20 is the easiest and most practical route to the Warbonnet battlefield. This will also take you to **Fort Robinson** in Nebraska, where Cody accompanied Sheridan prior to Warbonnet and where he sent his first report home following the skirmish. This is truly one of the great forts of the northern plains, encapsulated by today's Fort Robinson State Park. This is where the Oglala chief Crazy Horse was killed during his attempted arrest in 1877. This is also the site of the Cheyenne Outbreak of 1879, another of the tragic events of the Indian war. East of the park is the site of the original **Red Cloud Agency**, where Cody came in June and July 1876. (The modern-day Red Cloud Agency is today's Pine Ridge Reservation in South Dakota.)

Most of the post's original buildings still stand, framed in a somewhat dramatic setting by the buttes of the adjacent Pine Ridge. Quite a few of the officers' quarters and enlisted men's barracks are available for lodging, and an overnight (or longer) stay should be strongly considered—with the hiking, stagecoach and horseback rides, nature drives, golfing, swimming, buffalo stew cookouts, melodramas, two museums, nearby archaeology and geology parks, and more, you'll need a few days to accomplish everything.

A monument overlooking the Warbonnet battlefield commemorates Merritt's action.

Address: P.O. Box 392, Crawford, Nebraska 69339 (the fort is three miles west of Crawford). *Museum Hours:* Monday through Saturday, 8 A.M. to 5 P.M.; Sunday, 9 A.M. to 5 P.M. during the summer and 10 A.M. to 5 P.M. in the off-season. Closed weekends and holidays. *Admission:* Daily park permit is $5. Admission to Fort Robinson Museum is $2 for adults, free for children 18 and under. *Phone:* (308) 665-2919. *Websites:* www.ngpc.state.ne.us and www.nebraskahistory.org/sites/fortrob/.

The final stop is the Warbonnet battlefield. The easiest and most practical way to reach it is from Crawford. From the town, take Nebraska 2/71 north for twenty-eight miles, turning left onto Hat Creek Road at the state's border with South Dakota. Follow the all-weather road ten miles for a number of south and west turns until you reach the small Catholic church at the abandoned village of Montrose.

To the north of the church is the **Warbonnet Historic Site** (you'll see the sign). To the left is Hat Creek, where the Fifth Cavalry camped while waiting for the Cheyenne. The namesake Warbonnet Creek actually merges into the creek about three miles below the battle site.

You'll notice a large hill with a monument at the top and a half-mile trail headed toward it. This is the mound where Cody, Merritt, Carr, and others viewed the field; a seven-foot stone monument marks the spot. You'll also have seen the fenced-in stone marker to the right when you enter the battlefield. This is the location of Cody's killing of Yellow Hair. The stone monument was dedicated in 1934, placed by Cody's foster son, Johnny Baker, after interviews with Charles King and Christian Madsen. Baker, who started the project in 1920, died before the dedication, but his widow, Olive, attended, as did Madsen.

Recommended Reading

First Scalp for Custer: the Skirmish at Warbonnet Creek, Nebraska, July 17, 1876 by Paul L. Hedren (Lincoln: University of Nebraska Press, 1987); *Traveler's Guide to the Great Sioux War* by Paul L. Hedren (Helena: Montana Historical Society Press, 1996); *The Lives and Legends of Buffalo Bill* by Don Russell (Norman: University of Oklahoma Press, 1960).

Last Days as a Scout

Cody in 1876.

ody and the Fifth reached Fort Laramie from Camp Robinson on July 22, 1876, where word of Warbonnet and Cody's fight was first sent to the East. Even though it was a very small fight, it was thrilling news to the nation after Crook's standoff at the Rosebud and Custer's annihilation at Little Bighorn.

Resupplied, the column moved on to Fort Fetterman, arriving on July 25. There was no tarrying for the Fifth, which crossed the North Platte River the next morning. Cody and some of the officers hunted buffalo for rations before passing the sites of Fort Phil Kearny and the Fetterman massacre. They reached General Crook's camp on Goose Creek under the shadow of the Bighorn Mountains on August 3.

With the addition of the Fifth Cavalry, seven more infantry companies from Fort Fetterman, and some two hundred Shoshone Indians, Crook's column was again ready for the Sioux, with Merritt as its chief of cavalry and Carr resuming command of the Fifth. Given the title "Chief Scout," Cody headed about twenty civilian scouts, including the well-known Frank Grouard, Baptiste "Big Bat" Pourier, and John "Captain Jack" Crawford, the Poet Scout of the Black Hills.

Stripped for speed, with each man allowed a shelter half and a tin cup, Crook's column moved out on August 5. They reached the Tongue River

that day, working their way up its narrow canyon until reaching the divide between it and the Rosebud and crossing into that stream's valley in the Montana Territory. They arrived at Crook's Rosebud battlefield on the seventh, finding signs of Sioux camping there recently. Fields of grass had been burned off, leaving little for the massive column's horses and mules.

Cody rode ahead of Crook and found the command of Brig. Gen. Alfred Terry and the Seventh Cavalry on August 10. Both forces initially thought the other was the enemy until, as reported by 1st Lt. Edward S. Godfrey of the Seventh, "Bill Cody, *alias* 'Buffalo Bill,' rode up to our lines from Genl Crook's command."

The two wings of the 1876 Sioux campaign met on the Rosebud, about halfway between the

Gen. George Crook.

116

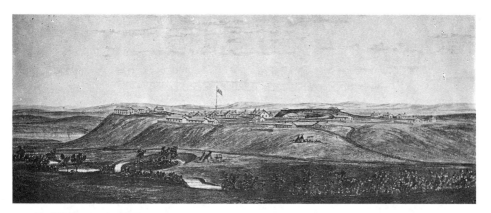

Fort Fetterman in 1870.

battle site and the stream's mouth on the Yellowstone. The combined forces moved north slowly along the Rosebud.

The plodding speed of the army gave Cody the opportunity to study and compare the commanders. "General Terry had his wagon train with him, and everything to make life comfortable on an Indian campaign," he wrote in his autobiography. "His camp looked very comfortable and attractive, and presented a great contrast to that of General Crook, who had for his headquarters only one small fly tent. . . . When I compared the two camps, I came to the conclusion that General Crook was an Indian fighter; for it was evident that he had learned that, to follow and fight Indians, a body of men must travel lightly and not be detained by a wagon train or heavy luggage of any kind."

There would be no opportunity to catch the Sioux that summer, as the Indian trail divided many times. Camp was made along the Yellowstone on August 17 to 24. Col. Nelson A. Miles and his Fifth Infantry accompanied Terry's column, but he was now going down the Yellowstone from the

The steamer **Far West,** *moored at the mouth of the Rosebud Creek on the Yellowstone.*

Captain Jack Crawford

John Crawford was born in 1847 in Donegal, Ireland, and arrived in America when he was a boy. He enlisted in the Forty-Eighth Pennsylvania Volunteers after coming of age (seventeen or eighteen), joining his father in the regiment. An injury at the Battle of Spotsylvania put him in a Philadelphia hospital, where one of the nurses taught him to read and write. Crawford returned to his regiment and was injured once again in Petersburg, with but a few short weeks before the war ended.

Crawford came west in 1875 and found work with the Omaha *Bee* as a correspondent during the earliest days of the Black Hills gold rush. In Custer City, he helped organize the Black Hills Rangers, serving as chief scout. He began to dress and wear his hair long like other scouts, and adopted the "Captain Jack" moniker out of the blue.

Unlike other scouts, however, Crawford led a life of abstinence after giving a deathbed oath to his mother to never drink. Such a virtue was appreciated by Buffalo Bill, who often drank. Cody met Crawford at Crook's Rosebud camp in August 1816. Crawford rode in with a gift for the man he had admired since seeing his show back home. "Jack informed me that he had brought me a present from Colonel Jones of Cheyenne," Cody recalled. "Jack Crawford is the only man I have ever known that could have brought that bottle of whiskey through without *accident* befalling it, for he is one of the very few teetotal scouts I ever met."

Jack was also one of the few scouts proficient in writing. Crawford reported for the Omaha *Bee* on the Black Hills gold rush and the Plains Indian wars. Besides his newspaper stories, Crawford wrote four books, three plays, and more than a hundred short stories. He was especially known for his poetry, leading to his nickname as the "Poet Scout" (and perhaps the founding father of "cowboy poetry").

The poems could be described as "sappy" by today's standards, but they struck a chord among Easterners for their romantic notions of the West and frontiersmen sentimental for lives left behind. Wild Bill Hickok once told Crawford (after hearing his poem "Mother's Prayers"), "You strike a tender spot, old boy, when you talk of mother that way."

Crawford scouted on the 1876 campaign, fighting the Sioux at the battle of Slim Buttes in Dakota and riding three hundred miles of dangerous territory to get news of the battle to the wire. He was reported to have killed and scalped a warrior, like Cody, but he never brought it up in his stage show, unlike Cody. He may have felt it would be imitating Buffalo Bill if he did, or that it was too

John "Captain Jack" Crawford in 1881.

gruesome to include. Or, as Louis Warren conjectured, it may have been that he never got the Indian's name.

Captain Jack was invited by Cody to join his Combination shows and, in fact, played Cody's Yellow Hand in Buffalo Bill's Warbonnet reenactment. Before the season was done, he was once again emulating Buffalo Bill in feeling he wasn't being paid his worth, just as Cody had felt under Buntline. (Cody began using Indians to play Indian roles after Crawford.)

When the scout was seriously injured in a stage mishap, and Cody didn't pay the hospital bill, Crawford decided to start his own company. That didn't sit well with Buffalo Bill, who angrily told that "had the accident not occurred I think you had (already) made up your mind to start out for yourself." Still, he wished Jack success and vowed to never retaliate against him.

That didn't hold for Crawford, who now saw Cody as his lifelong rival, inasmuch as a nail rivals a hammer. He publicly disparaged Cody, once writing that "Ned Buntline created the most selfish and brutal fake hero ever perpetrated on the American people." He continued jealously sniping at his former friend as Buffalo Bill's shows grew and prospered while Crawford's fame and fortune proved elusive.

Jack mellowed over the years, however. As he lay on his deathbed in New York, he heard that Cody had preceded him and supposedly said: "So Bill Cody is gone? I guess they will be sounding taps over me pretty soon. Well, when we meet Tall Bull and that tough old codger Sitting Bull on the other side and stick up our hands palm forward and say, 'How Kola!' there will be a lot to talk about." He died on February 28, 1917, seven weeks after his one-time hero.

Recommended Reading

Ho! For the Black Hills: Captain Jack Crawford Reports the Black Hills Gold Rush and Great Sioux War by Paul Hedren (Pierre: South Dakota State Historical Society Press, 2012).

Officers' row at Fort Buford, around 1881. NATIONAL ARCHIVES

mouth of the Powder River aboard the steamer *Far West*, with Cody along to scout from its pilot house. This presented the opportunity to meet the riverboat's famed captain, Grant Marsh.

No Indians were spotted on the trip up to the mouth of the Glendive Creek, where Grant shored the *Far West* for the night. Miles needed dispatches delivered to Terry at once, and Cody said, "At his request I took the dispatches and rode seventy-five miles that night through the bad lands of the Yellowstone, and reached General Terry's camp next morning, after having nearly broken my neck a dozen times or more."

Seeing few prospects of any more Indian fighting that summer, Cody resolved to return to the theater circuit. His complaints were heard by a newsman for the *Chicago Tribune:* "He said plainly that the soldiers did not want or intend to fight, that he had worn himself out finding Indians; and, when he did discover their whereabouts, there was no one ready to 'go for them.'" A trooper in the Third Cavalry, Oliver C. C. Pollock of Troop M, said it was likely a different reason: "[W]e saw Buffalo Bill and his black horse leave on a supply boat. He was sore because Frank Grouard proved he knew the country better than Bill, and Grouard's advice was taken."

In any event, Cody was discharged on August 22 as Merritt's chief of scouts. During his trip down the Yellowstone aboard the steamer of the same name, Cody met with Texas Jack Omohundro, who was on his way upstream as a correspondent for the *New York Herald.* Cody was talked into carrying more dispatches between Gen. Joseph Whistler, also aboard the *Yellowstone*, and General Terry. Much like his Pony Express days, he reported making incredible rides of great distances, over rough terrain, in dangerous lands, and with little rest. He even turned down offers of pay.

Terry again took Cody on as a scout, sending him ahead to the army stockade at Glendive. Cody dodged some Indians on a buffalo hunt during the trek before his arrival, then went back to guide the column into the camp. When he got there, the *Far West* was preparing to move downstream to Fort Buford. Cody joined it, taking the boat as far as Bismarck, where he took the train to Chicago and eventually home to Rochester. His last paid day as a scout was September 6, 1876.

The Trail Today

There's little left of the Fort Fetterman that Buffalo Bill Cody saw in 1876. After the post was abandoned in 1882, most of the buildings were taken or stripped of their wood, doors, and windows. Two buildings, the officers' quarters and ordnance storehouse, survived and were restored as the centerpieces of **Fort Fetterman State Historic Site**, northwest of Douglas, Wyoming. The visitor center within the officers' quarters includes exhibits, artifacts, and a video to tell the story of the fort, but walk the site to truly experience the exposure and loneliness soldiers must have felt at this

An officers' quarters serves as the visitor center for Fort Fetterman State Historic Site.

This 1908 monument commemorates the Fetterman Massacre, the greatest defeat of the U.S. Army until Little Bighorn.

dreary western outpost. *Address:* 752 Highway 93, Douglas, Wyoming 82633 (Exit 140 off Interstate 25). *Hours:* Open daily from Memorial Day to Labor Day, with buildings open from 9 A.M. to 5 P.M. and grounds open from dawn to dusk. Closed during winter months. *Admission:* Wyoming residents $2, nonresidents $4, children 17 and under free. *Phone:* (307) 358-9288. *Website:* wyoparks.state.wy.us/Site/SiteInfo.aspx?siteID=19 (or google "Fort Fetterman").

By the time Cody and the Fifth reached the site of old Fort Phil Kearny, it was long gone, destroyed by Indians after its abandonment eight years earlier. The state of Wyoming recreated a portion of its stockade with the establishment of **Fort Phil Kearny State Historic Site**, along with an interpretive trail around the grounds of the old fort. The visitor center includes a small museum with artifacts and a diorama, as well as a fine bookstore. *Address:* 528 Wagon Box Road, Banner, Wyoming 82832 (Exit 44 off Interstate 90). *Hours:* Visitor center, May 1 through September 30, 8 A.M. to 6 P.M.; October 1 through May 14, noon to 4 P.M. Grounds open year round. *Admission:* Wyoming residents $2, nonresidents $4, children 17 and under free. *Phone:* (307) 684-7629. *Website:* www.fortphilkearny.com.

Two miles from the fort on the abandoned Highway 87 is the **Fetterman Massacre Monument**. One of the unique events at Fort Phil Kearny is the anniversary tour of the battlefield held every December 21, regardless of the weather. On that date in 1866, around eighty soldiers commanded by Capt. William Fetterman were surprised and annihilated by more than two thousand Sioux, Northern Cheyenne, and Arapaho. Until the Little Bighorn fight nearly ten years later, it was the largest defeat of U.S. forces in the Plains Indian wars. Contact the fort for more information.

Crook's Goose Creek camp is in the heart of today's Sheridan, located near the junction of Lewis, Dow, and Alger Streets and across from Mill Park. While in Sheridan, also take note of another Buffalo Bill site. The **Sheridan Inn** at 856 Broadway was the first establishment in his W. F. Cody Hotel Company, with Cody owning the business rather than the property.

The Sheridan Inn, once home to tryouts for Buffalo Bill's Wild West, today sits idle after its restoration.

He frequently visited the 1893 property and often held auditions for the Wild West show on the front lawn of the many-gabled hotel—likely quite a thrill for railroad passengers who would have seen it as their trains pulled into the station. The Sheridan Inn continued as a hotel but saw a number of owners come and go through the 1960s. The property was rumored to be slated for demolition in 1965 until painter and heiress Neltje Doubleday Kings bought the inn, renovated it, and operated it for nearly twenty years. After she donated it to a non-profit, the Sheridan was sold, went bankrupt, and was turned over to another non-profit that operated it for a few years until it was closed in 2012. The Sheridan Inn has reopened under new ownership. Keep track of its activities at www.sheridaninn.com.

Cody saw the site of Crook's battle with the Sioux and Cheyenne on the Rosebud Creek about a month and a half after the fight. You can see it today at the **Rosebud Battlefield State Park**, an undeveloped park about forty miles north of Sheridan via Wyoming Highway 338 and Montana Highway 314. There are a few historical and interpretive markers to aid your visit, along with picnic tables and primitive restrooms. It is a beautiful site and worth the drive. *Hours:* Open year round. *Admission:* Non-Montana residents $5. *Phone:* (406) 234-0900. *Website:* stateparks.mt.gov/rosebud-battlefield. (The much more heavily visited Little Bighorn Battlefield National Monument is nearby, about forty-five miles to the northwest via Montana 314 and U.S. 212.)

Cody's route with Crook took him through the Rosebud Valley to the Yellowstone River. You can travel it, for the most part, by taking Montana 314 north to Busby, U.S. 212 east to Lame Deer, and Montana 447 north to Rosebud. If you drive from Rosebud to Glendive via Interstate 94, you'll

Among the reconstructed buildings at Fort Buford State Historic Site is the Brotherton Quarters, the site of Sitting Bull's surrender.

see more of the Montana scenery that Buffalo Bill saw from his riverboat runs. After boarding the *Far West* at the Glendive Stockade, he soon crossed the border into the Dakota Territory for a stop at Fort Buford.

Fort Buford State Historic Site features several original and reconstructed buildings, including an enlisted barracks, powder magazine, and the Brotherton Quarters, site of Sitting Bull's 1881 surrender. The state of North Dakota has added to this site—where two great rivers join—with the **Missouri-Yellowstone Confluence Interpretive Center**. This modern facility serves not only as the visitor center for the fort but also as a museum for the area, with displays on Lewis and Clark, wildlife, the fur trade, Indian artifacts, and artwork. *Address:* 15349 39th Lane Northwest, Williston, North Dakota 58801 (about twenty-two miles southwest of Williston). *Hours:* Open daily May 16 to September 15, 8 A.M. to 6 P.M.; September 16 to May 15, 9 A.M. to 4 P.M.; Wednesday to Saturday, 1 to 5 P.M. Sunday. *Admission:* Adults $5, children $2.50. *Phone:* (701) 572-9034. *Website:* www.history.nd.gov/ historicsites/buford.

The Impresario Rancher

Buffalo Bill in the late 1870s.

At the end of 1876, Cody had to realize that the Indian wars would soon end, and with them opportunities to scout for the army. It was a young man's game (he was now thirty), and the entertainment business was so much easier and more profitable. For the five years after his last days as a scout, Cody toured the U.S. and Europe with the Buffalo Bill Combination as an impresario/entertainer.

The task was made easier with new material collected on the Plains, particularly the successful "battle" at Warbonnet Creek. The incident figured into his performances with the Buffalo Bill Combination, and the bloody souvenirs he collected from Yellow Hair were used to promote the shows. (After some considerable protest from those who saw the public display of the scalp and warbonnet as too gruesome, Cody removed them and placed them within the performance hall. People who wanted to see them now had to come to the show.)

Still, Cody announced in 1877 that the year's Buffalo Bill Combination was to be a farewell tour before he returned to Nebraska—"to remain there the rest of his life as a cattle dealer and gentleman farmer," reported a newspaper. It's not known if that was a ruse to ensure sold-out performances or if Cody really did plan to become a cattle baron.

It does appear that he had plans for it. On the way to San Francisco, Cody called on Frank North in Sidney, Nebraska, where the Pawnee Scouts were mustered out. Cody proposed to North, whose days as a scout were now ended as well, that he and the North brothers go into the cattle business with him. It seemed to be a sure bet to buy feeder cattle, graze them on public land, and sell them at a hefty profit. The brothers agreed, and the Cody–North partnership was created.

North found land at the headwaters of the South Fork of the Dismal River, about sixty-five miles north of North Platte. This was open range—they could claim it and build their ranch house and other structures on it, but they didn't own the land. It was deeper into the Sand Hills than other ranchers had ventured, but it was well watered and well grassed. They bought cattle at Ogallala (then the north end of the Texas cattle trail) and drove them to the ranch. North hired the cowboys and operated the ranch while Cody continued to tour and perform.

Most ranchers saw Cody as a "gentleman farmer," in that it was not his focus and he did not engage in the work. Cody himself wrote: "As there is nothing but hard work on these round-ups, having to be in the saddle all day, and standing guard over the cattle at night, rain or shine, I could not possibly find out where the fun came in that North had promised me."

But he enjoyed having a ranch, frequently bringing out family, friends, VIPs, and celebrities to enjoy good times with the cowboys. John Bratt, who later bought out the Cody–North ranching interests, wrote in his book, *Trails of Yesterday*, that Cody's freewheeling demeanor found favor with the help. "[S]ome of the cowboys would take advantage of the Colonel's hospitality by going to his wagon and helping themselves to his cigars and sampling his liquors that had been brought along as an antidote against snake bites and other accidents." The cowboys, always eager to show the owner a good time, also put on bronco-riding, roping, racing, wild steer-riding, and swimming contests, as well as friendly poker games for the entertainment of Cody.

The Cody and North Ranch operation survived until 1882. By that time, homesteaders had moved into the open range and took the best of the surrounding grazing land. As Cody now had four thousand acres at North Platte, the Dismal River ranch was no longer necessary, and the Cody–North partnership was dissolved.

The 1877–1878 tour of the Buffalo Bill Combination began in Omaha in late June, followed by stops in the western states of California, Oregon, Nevada, and Utah before disbanding in Omaha. It was back in Omaha that simmering differences between Bill and Lulu took a new turn.

After paying off the actors for the season and buying drinks all around, Cody prepared to leave a celebration party. The four actresses in the company (according to his divorce testimony) "all jumped up and they said, 'Papa, we want to kiss you good bye.' They called me papa, the ladies did in the company that season, and I kissed them good bye and we were all laughing and joking." Lulu, meanwhile, was in their room down the hall, getting angrier and angrier. Bill never did understand why.

Detail from a postcard printed for the Cody and North Ranch, showing the placement of the ranch's brand on livestock. "BUFFALO TOM" MARTENS, COLUMBUS, NEBRASKA

In early fall, Cody returned to the Red Cloud Agency to hire "real" Indians for his show; previously, actors or people off the street had been hired to play Indians. For the 1878–79 show, Cody went to the Pawnee Reservation in the Indian Territory (now Oklahoma) and hired a band for the show.

His hiring of Indians came to the attention of the Commissioner of Indian Affairs, who was concerned that Cody was taking advantage of the Indians, in addition to removing those who were essentially "wards" of the U.S. government, without authority. Cody successfully argued that he was showing the Indians the customs and the people of the United States while touring with them so that they might share that knowledge with their people. (He could also have mentioned, but didn't, that he was providing them with much-needed income.) That argument sat well with the Bureau of Indian Affairs, which made Cody a special Indian agent and committed him to return the Indians to their reservation at the end of their contracts.

The touring continued until 1882. Although still profitable, the Buffalo Bill Combination was not the production that Cody realized was possible for a production of the West. An opportunity came the following year in his new hometown of North Platte.

The Trail Today

When Buffalo Bill met with Frank North in Sidney in 1877, it was still one of the wildest towns of the west. Founded in 1867 as an end-of-the-line settlement by the Union Pacific during construction of the transcontinental railroad, Sidney was also home to Sidney Barracks (later Fort Sidney), and by 1877 it was one end of the historic Sidney–Black Hills gold trail, which gave it an ever-churning population of soldiers, gold seekers, shippers, emigrants, rail workers, gamblers, saloon floozies, and gunfighters. It was an exciting place, and Buffalo Bill was said to have visited often.

Cody surely would have passed through Fort Sidney, of which there are remnants within the **Fort Sidney Complex**. An 1884 officers' quarters is now home to the Cheyenne County Historical Museum, containing artifacts from both the fort and the county's early settlers, and the nearby 1871 commanding officer's home holds a diorama of the post and period furnishings; free tours are offered of both buildings. *Address:* Sixth and Jackson Streets, Sidney, Nebraska 69162. *Hours:* Day after Memorial Day through Labor Day, Monday to Friday, 9 to 11 A.M. and 1 to 3 P.M.; Saturday and Sunday, 1 to 4 P.M. *Admission:* Free. *Phone:* (308) 254-2150.

Cody attended services at the **Christ Episcopal Church** (1205 10th Avenue), built as the original church of Fort Sidney in 1886. He was also

Today the original officers' quarters of Fort Sidney serves as home of the Cheyenne County Historical Museum in Sidney.

Sidney's Christ Episcopal Church was attended—and apparently vandalized—by William F. Cody.

said to have carved his name into one of the pews of the church, but another parishioner, outraged at this vandalism many years later, decided to fill, sand, and restain the carving, which can't be found today.

Unmarked and on private land, the **Cody and North Ranch** was situated to the north of today's McPherson–Hooker county line. To reach the

The original Cody and North Ranch house is today located at Cody's Scout's Rest Ranch.

general vicinity of their ranch, starting at the McPherson county seat of
Tryon, drive west on Nebraska 92 for fifteen miles to Soddy Road. Take this
road north for about fourteen miles (crossing the county line) to enter the
valley of the South Fork of the Dismal River and the grazing land of the
ranch. Unbelievably, the original log cabin constructed on the Dismal River
for the Cody and North Ranch still stands and is available for public viewing. The cabin was moved several times to other Sand Hills ranches before
it was dismantled and reassembled at Cody's Scout's Rest Ranch in North
Platte (see next chapter).

North Platte: Home on the Plains

Cody, Louisa, and their nine-year-old daughter Arta before their move to North Platte.

ven though Rochester, New York, was close to the entertainment centers of the East, the Codys were destined to return to the Plains. Cody wanted to get into the lucrative business of cattle ranching, and Louisa was tired of traveling, despite still harboring suspicions of her husband's philandering. They may also have wanted to remove themselves from the heartbreak of Kit's burial in Rochester.

North Platte, Nebraska, was a natural selection as a new "hometown." Both were very familiar with North Platte, given that it was only fifteen miles from Fort McPherson, where Cody had been stationed as a scout. It would also put him in proximity to his ranch with Frank North, located some sixty-five miles to the north of town.

Cody bought his first land in North Platte in 1878—$750 for 160 acres south of the Union Pacific tracks and west of the Post at North Platte Station, the small military camp there. In the years to come, Cody would purchase nearly 4,000 acres, mostly north of the tracks. (In reality, and unknown to Cody, most of the property was in Louisa's name. Not trusting his freewheeling ways and having some business sense of her own, she decided to buy the property in her name alone when he sent the money home.)

Louisa and the Codys' daughters moved to North Platte in February 1878 to supervise the construction of a home on their new farm, taking

The Post at North Platte Station, which was deactivated shortly before the Codys' relocation to the town. Louisa and their daughter likely lived in the nearest structure while their home was built.

temporary lodging in the officers' headquarters of the recently abandoned military post. Their new home was done by the time Cody got there in May, although he spent most of the summer at the Cody and North Ranch at the Dismal River.

Not much is known of this first house, other than the Codys called it the "Welcome Wigwam." It was a story and a half tall, a large house for North Platte but soon outpaced as people and money began to accumulate in the town. The Codys were prominent North Platters themselves, with Bill's celebrity and Lulu's growing stature as a real-estate investor. Instead of retiring to ranching as once planned, Bill continued to tour and perform, sending money home to Louisa to buy more property.

Cody's autobiography was produced in 1879. How much of it was written by Cody and how much of it was factual cannot be determined. His original account may have been much more factual before an editor's handling. As was mentioned earlier, some parts were obvious fabrications to build up the life of Buffalo Bill and to substantiate some of his theatrical portrayals, while some were poignant stories of a boy growing up on the Plains. Regardless, the book was very popular and increased Buffalo Bill's exposure. It was a best-seller in North Platte as well, where his thirteen-year-old daughter "Miss Arta Cody is canvassing the city to sell the book, a work which will meet with a ready sale wherever offered," reported the local news. The price: $2.50 for leather, $2 for cloth.

Cody was in North Platte in the spring of 1882, visiting with a former mayor and other prominent citizens at a local store, when he asked what the town had planned for the Fourth of July. After he was told there was nothing scheduled, he left mumbling about being surprised that the town would do so little. He soon walked back in, complaining that it was unpatriotic not to celebrate the national holiday, and it was soon suggested that he was just the man to chair such a celebration.

Cody had an idea to run cattle around the town's racetrack while firing blanks to demonstrate how a buffalo hunt worked. A friend who owned some buffalo suggested they be used instead. Local businesses were persuaded to offer prizes—along with those provided by Cody—for shooting, riding, and bronco busting, as well as other contests thought of interest to the local cowboys. The prizes and games were printed up on handbills and sent to ranches for miles around. The promotion worked. Cody hoped for a hundred cowboys, and more than a thousand turned out.

Cody's show began at 10:30 on the morning of the Fourth with a parade down Main Street. There was a band, followed by veterans of the Grand Army of the Republic, then children of North Platte, townspeople, and carriages, all headed for the track. They held the cowboy contests, along with

Buffalo Bill's new Scout's Rest Ranch, depicted in an 1888 supplement to the North Platte
Telegraph.

speeches and singing, and the evening events included fireworks and a
GAR Ball.

They called the Independence Day festival the "Old Glory Blow-Out,"
and it was a huge success. People came from miles around, with one account
saying the countryside was emptied for a one hundred and fifty-mile radius.
Others had proposed similar events or carried out some of its elements, but
the Old Glory Blow-Out was one of the first rodeos in the country. Because
of its success, it spurred Cody to create an even more spectacular presentation the following year, which eventually became Buffalo Bill's Wild West
(see next chapter).

That next year, 1883, was one of joy, sadness, and continued strife
between the Codys. Their daughter Irma was born in North Platte in February, but their eleven-year-old daughter Orra died in October. She was
buried alongside her brother in Rochester.

Problems between Cody and Louisa were growing. He was always a
drinker, but now he was drinking even more. She had always nagged him
and was doing so more. They both had their suspicions of the other: he
thought she was destroying him financially, and she doubted his fidelity.
Orra's death came at a time Cody considered divorcing Louisa and it probably led to even more drinking.

But the money continued to pour in. Flush with cash from successful
touring, Cody decided in 1886 to build a ranch home north of town and at

the south end of the four thousand acres he had accumulated. He wanted a showcase to which he'd eventually retire, and for that reason called it the Scout's Rest Ranch. He convinced his sister Julia Goodman to design the home (basically copying another French Second Empire-style in town) and her husband, Al, to operate the ranch, which would include high-grade livestock and thoroughbred horses.

The words "Scout's Rest Ranch" were painted on the roof of the barn, the lettering large enough to be seen from the Union Pacific tracks a mile away. Guests frequently called on Bill at the ranch, from visiting VIPs to Wild West performers, fellow retired scouts, local friends, and cowboys.

Bill and Louisa were living separately at this point in their respective houses, but this was not to be the last Cody home in North Platte. The first Welcome Wigwam burned to the ground in 1891; the second Welcome Wigwam came about because of another run-in between Bill and Lulu, this one during the World's Columbian Exposition in Chicago. She came to the city without calling ahead in order to surprise Bill, but when she asked to be taken to his room (not identifying herself), the front desk told her she'd be shown to "Mr. and Mrs. Cody's room." Lulu had already heard rumors of an actress associated with her husband, and this apparent confirmation was naturally upsetting.

To smooth the waters, he bought her the finest home in North Platte—a highly ornate, three-story mansion featuring an open stairway, library,

A public notice of the W. F. Cody brand (a pipe) identifies his ranch land between the North Platte and South Platte Rivers.

Postcard of the second "Welcome Wigwam" home, purchased for Louisa Cody in 1893.

sitting room, fireplaces, and many bedrooms. The new Welcome Wigwam became her home for the next sixteen years, and the Codys' daughter Irma was married here in 1903.

It was to North Platte that Cody always returned to restore himself from the exhaustion of touring. A local newspaper wrote in 1898 that all he had to do was "visit his family, look after his extensive interests, shake hands with all his friends and recuperate his health." He spent money freely on North Platte, particularly after the windfall of performing at the Columbian Exposition in Chicago. He bought the town band the most expensive uniforms they could find. Each of the churches in North Platte received five hundred dollars, and another report says Cody paid off the debts of five of the churches, gave each pastor a year's living, and donated land for the cemetery and fairgrounds. It was said any boy who opened the door for Buffalo Bill to a local saloon would be sure to get a five-dollar tip.

There had to have been some heartbreak, therefore, when Cody announced in 1901 that he had given up his legal residence in North Platte and was relocating to Cody, Wyoming, a town he'd helped found. Louisa continued to live in North Platte, and he initiated divorce proceedings in 1905. For a time he did not visit North Platte, feeling that the town was probably against him in the split-up. The Codys lived in North Platte for about twenty-five years, the longest they ever lived anywhere. Buffalo Bill continued to visit, however, checking on his ranch and visiting old friends, before he and Louisa eventually reconciled after a visit orchestrated by a grandson.

The Trail Today

While the first Welcome Wigwam was under construction, Lulu and Orra lived for a short while in the **officers' quarters at the Post at North Platte Station**. The last of the troops left in November 1877, just a couple of months before the Codys moved in, but the army continued to own the buildings until 1881. In that year, they were sold off, and the land was platted for lots.

There were two buildings identified as "officers' quarters" in a drawing of the post, and it's believed that one of them survives today. This building (also identified as the post surgeon's quarters) became a private residence at 314 West Sixth Street after the post was closed. The home now has a porch and an addition in the back, but it is still recognizable when compared to an early photograph of the structure. There's no way of telling whether Louisa and Orra lived here or in the other officers' quarters, but with its original construction in 1869, it may well be the oldest home in North Platte.

The **first Welcome Wigwam** was at the northwest corner of West Sixth and Sherman Streets. Cody's financial hardships after the 1911 season forced him to liquidate much of his holdings, and he broke up the original one hundred and sixty acres into lots and acre tracts in 1912. He also named the new streets after the officers under whom he had once served—

This house at 314 West Sixth Street in North Platte was the post surgeon's quarters from the Post at North Platte Station. It once neighbored the quarters where Louisa Cody lived.

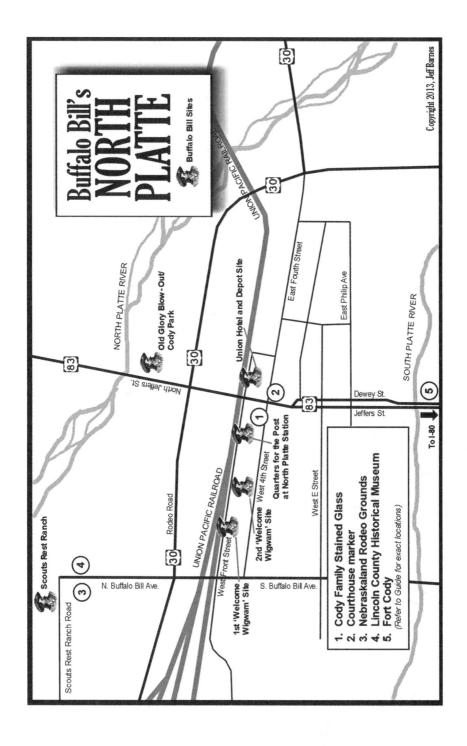

Buffalo Bill's NORTH PLATTE

Buffalo Bill Sites

Copyright 2013, Jeff Barnes

1. Cody Family Stained Glass
2. Courthouse marker
3. Nebraskaland Rodeo Grounds
4. Lincoln County Historical Museum
5. Fort Cody
(Refer to Guide for exact locations)

Sherman, Sheridan, Miles, Carr, Custer, Emory, Hayes, and Mills, whose names still grace those streets today.

The **second Welcome Wigwam** was on the north side of West Fourth Street between Washington and Adams Streets and was sold by Mrs. Cody in 1912. After Cody died in 1917, some North Platte residents talked of buying the old estate and creating a Buffalo Bill museum. The town wasn't interested enough, however; the home was torn down in 1930 and replaced by a modern residence, using some of the original home's materials.

In downtown North Platte, on the front of the **Lincoln County Courthouse** at East Fourth and Jeffers Streets, is a bronze plaque for the Old Glory Blow-Out featuring a bas-relief portrait of Buffalo Bill. The parade marched past this spot in 1883.

Near the courthouse, at West Fourth and Vine Streets, is the Episcopal Church of Our Savior, within which is a very interesting piece of Cody memorabilia: the **Cody Family stained glass**, a gift to the church by his daughter Arta in 1894. The glass features the full-size depictions of her deceased siblings Orra and Kit under the protective arms of Jesus . . . who bears a strong likeness to her father, William F. Cody. The original church in which the glass was located was destroyed by fire in 1962, but the glass survived and was installed in the new church's St. George Chapel.

The **site of the Union Pacific Hotel and Depot** is next to the U.P. track, behind the Alco store and two blocks east of the U.S. 83 viaduct on Front Street. It was here that Buffalo Bill welcomed Sheridan, Custer, and Grand Duke Alexis to North Platte before leaving on the most famous buffalo hunt the world had ever known. This was also where the Codys made most of their arrivals and departures while North Platte was home.

The original depot burned down in 1915 and was replaced by another depot, earning considerable fame during World War II as the site of the North Platte Canteen, which fed and entertained six million servicemen and women passing through the city during the war. That building was demolished by the Union Pacific in the 1970s, and the railroad replaced it with the historic plaza now at the site.

The stained glass featuring Cody's deceased children and a familiar-looking face depicted as Jesus.

Cody's French Second Empire home at Scout's Rest Ranch.

Across the viaduct, one mile north on Jeffers Street/U.S. 83, is **Cody Park**. At the park's entrance is the Wild West Memorial to the cowboys, Indian, riders, ropers, and other individuals who made the show a success, with an avenue of flags representing the states and nations which hosted Buffalo Bill's Wild West. Within the gazebo is a lifesize statue of Cody, a gift from the people of Great Britain.

Passing through this city park (home to amusement rides, outdoor activities, and Union Pacific engines), you'll reach a large pond with birds and wildlife. In 1882, this pond was a racing track and the site of the Old Glory Blow-Out.

Return south on U.S. 83, then right (west) on old U.S. 30, and then north on Buffalo Bill Avenue. You'll see the signs and soon encounter the **Buffalo Bill Ranch State Historical Park**. The white mansion with green trim stands out, but not more than the huge barn that still says "SCOUT'S REST RANCH" on its roof.

Scout's Rest Ranch was part of Cody's liquidation efforts and was sold to his show partner

Den with Cody's traveling desk.

Gordon "Pawnee Bill" Lillie for $100,000. The Cody family lived there until April 1913, when they moved to Cody, Wyoming. The State of Nebraska acquired the property in 1960 and created the state park. The house, barn, and original outbuildings are now maintained by the Nebraska Game and Parks Commission.

This is a must-see stop on the Cody Trail, starting with a tour of his home. The tour incorporates Cody's den (just inside the front door), dining room, sitting room, a guest room, and rooms for Irma, Louisa, and Buffalo Bill himself. The home is decorated to the period and incorporates many of the Codys' possessions, including his leather chair, the desk he used in his tent and railway car, and the bed used in his private room at the Irma Hotel in Cody, Wyoming. A renovation in 1909 added additional rooms to the house for extra guests and staff. Today this space holds memorabilia from Cody's life, such as his commission as colonel from the Nebraska governor, firearms and clothing from his Wild West shows, his wide-brimmed hat, medals, photographs, and much, much more.

Dominating the grounds is the ranch's massive barn. Built in 1887, this is distinctly a Buffalo Bill structure. Besides the large "Scout's Rest Ranch" painted on the shingles and the cupola bearing the name "Col. W. F. Cody," the barn features inverted aces of spades at the peak of both ends of the barn. This was to recognize Annie Oakley and her trick of firing a shot through that particular card. The clever woodworking continues on the eaves of the barn where each (seventy-three per side) is carved into the shape of a gunstock. The interior of the barn includes posters of Cody's

The barn dominates the grounds at Scout's Rest Ranch, with its roof lettering visible for a mile.

Fort Cody Trading Post at the interstate entrance to North Platte.

productions over the years—on one wall, peeling posters are pasted one after the other. It's said that Cody himself put up the advertisements after returning to Scout's Rest Ranch at the end of every season.

Related Attractions

For a well-rounded Buffalo Bill experience in North Platte, you have to stop at the **Fort Cody Trading Post**, a souvenir shop on steroids at the main entrance to the city on the Lincoln Highway from Interstate 80 at the U.S. 83 exit. You can't miss seeing it (it's configured like a stockaded frontier fort with a giant Buffalo Bill in the parking lot), and you shouldn't miss the inside either.

Beyond offering just about any kitschy Old West souvenir you could ever want, Fort Cody has a wonderful bookstore and a fine little museum loaded with vintage cowboy gear and U.S. cavalry and Indian wars items. The highlight is a truly incredible piece of folk art: the twenty thousand-piece Buffalo Bill's Wild West in miniature. Cody, Annie Oakley, cowboys, Indians, kids in the stands—they're all here, carved by hand; every thirty minutes, the motorized portion of the show begins. *Address:* 221 Halligan Drive, North Platte, Nebraska 69101. *Hours:* Summer—open daily from 9 A.M. to 9 P.M. Labor Day to Memorial Day—Monday to Saturday, 9 A.M. to 5:30 P.M.; Sunday, noon to 5:30 P.M. *Phone:* (308) 532-8081. *Website:* www.fortcody.com.

Recommended Reading

Buffalo Bill: His Family, Friends, Fame, Failures, and Fortunes by Nellie Snyder Yost (Chicago: Sage Book, 1979).

The Birth of the Wild West

Buffalo Bill Cody in the 1880s.
KANSAS HISTORICAL SOCIETY

The success of the Old Glory Blow-Out convinced Cody that an exhibition portraying the excitement and color of the West would be the next path of his career. The Buffalo Bill Combination would continue for a few more years, but his energy would be devoted to the creation of the new production.

In 1882, before the North Platte event, Cody met with promoter Nate Salsbury to discuss such a presentation for Europe. Salsbury went to Europe for research but came back unconvinced it would be profitable, at least for the present. Cody, meanwhile, continued to tour with the Combination while raising capital for a Wild West project.

During his planning, Cody met Dr. W. F. Carver, a trick-shooting dentist who called himself the "Evil Spirit of the Plains." Don Russell wrote that nothing seems to be known of Carver's life on the Plains except what he had said himself—and his stories seldom agreed with his earlier tellings. But Cody was impressed enough with Carver to engage him as a partner and brought him from Connecticut to Nebraska.

Cody wanted the presentation to be authentic and assembled cowboys, scouts, and Indians as talent for the show. He had buffalo, a pair of elk, mountain sheep, wild horses and saddle horses, and even a team of New-foundland dogs trained to pull a small covered wagon. A stagecoach was purchased from the Cheyenne and Black Hills stage line (famously known as the "Deadwood coach"), and covered wagons and other equipment were collected. He paraded the whole menagerie through downtown North Platte to the stockyards and the depot and boarded it all on six boxcars.

The new venture required some rehearsal before presentation to the people of Omaha, the first scheduled stop. A nat-ural site for the rehearsal was the east-central town of Columbus, Nebraska, at the confluence of the Platte and Loup Rivers.

Columbus had a number of things going for it. It was an easy day's travel by rail to Omaha, allowing time needed to load and unload the train. Additionally, it was the hometown of Cody's ranching partner Frank North, who could pro-vide the local services, people, and Pawnee Indi-ans needed for preparation of the show. Finally, North's brother James was president of the

W. F. "Doc" Carver.

Columbus Driving Park and Fair Association and could provide the space for the rehearsal.

(Both Russell and Nellie Snyder Yost erroneously state that Columbus was known as "Colville" at the time of the rehearsal. Columbus was incorporated in 1858 and always existed under that name, while Colville was a post office in Sioux County that lasted from 1907 to 1908. The only connection that Colville and Columbus seem to have is that one follows the other in an alphabetical listing of Nebraska towns.)

The rehearsal went on for about a week without incident save for the following questionable story. The mayor and town council members were riding in the Deadwood stagecoach, pulled by a team of barely broken mules, when it was "attacked" by a war band of Pawnees. The mules bolted and ran out of control as the Indians chased them and the dignitaries shouted for them to stop. By the time the mules tired out and the stagecoach halted, the mayor, thinking he was set up, was ready to strangle Cody. But the story lacks authenticity: it wasn't documented at the time and was first reported only many years later.

By May 16, 1883, the company was ready for Omaha. The train left Columbus, and "The Wild West, Hon. W. F. Cody and Dr. W. F. Carver's Rocky Mountain and Prairie Exhibition" was on its way.

More than twenty-five years passed before Cody made his way back to Columbus with the exhibition that became known as "Buffalo Bill's Wild West" (although he brought the Buffalo Bill Combination to town in 1886). His return would be for a performance of Buffalo Bill's Wild West and Pawnee Bill's Far East, which came in on September 3, 1909. Besides providing entertainment for the town, Cody also led a long-overdue memorial service for his partner and friend Frank North, who died in 1885 (see the sidebar on pages 73–74). So many people turned out for the service that it was held in the town's opera house.

An even larger crowd assembled at the Columbus Cemetery for the military services held for Major North. To honor their deceased fellow player, all of the show's performers attended in full costume, along with the cowboys and the Indians in their war paint and feathers; members of the military filed into the procession to the cemetery. Both Cody and Pawnee Bill (Gordon W. Lillie) spoke at North's grave for their departed friend. Cody also left flowers at the nearby graves of Wild West members George Clother and Fred Matthews, the latter of whom had been the driver of the Deadwood stagecoach.

Besides this solemn event and the business of putting on a production, Cody also had the opportunity to socialize in Columbus, revisiting the saloons he likely patronized during the 1883 rehearsal. Bucher's Saloon

Bucher's Saloon, right, in a rare photo from the early 1880s, the same time period of Buffalo Bill's possible first visit to the tavern. The building at the left is Columbus's opera house, site of Frank North's funeral service in 1885. "BUFFALO TOM" MARTENS, COLUMBUS, NEBRASKA

was one. A local legend, which first appeared in print in 1974 and is undocumented, says he slapped a thousand-dollar bill on the bar to buy drinks for everyone in the saloon, causing the bar owner to nearly faint.

The 1909 show drew people from near and far. Trains poured in with customers from surrounding communities and left others behind. The show grounds were inadequate for the crowd; Cody told a friend in town that the ticket sales for the afternoon performance totaled ten to eleven thousand dollars. The response was enough to bring the production back to Columbus again in 1912, 1914, and 1915.

The Trail Today

There are a number of landmarks associated with Buffalo Bill that still exist in Columbus, with only the largest changing beyond recognition.

The **old county fairgrounds**, the birthplace of Buffalo Bill's Wild West, was once a mile northwest of the town but is now a housing addition. At best, you can drive to 31st Street and 33rd Avenue (the southeast corner of the grounds), look to the northwest, and imagine Bill and his performers going through their performance routines.

The **graves of Frank and Luther North** are on the east side of town. Enter the Columbus Cemetery at 11th Street and 12th Avenue (streets run

Frank North's grave, visited by Buffalo Bill and several hundred others in 1909.

east–west, avenues north–south), make a right, then a left, and you'll soon spot the twin-columned marble and granite marker of Frank and his wife, Mary (who died two years before him). Luther's grave is to the right, while the graves of Wild West performers George Clother and Fred Matthews are nearby to the northwest, with George Turner farther to the northeast. Other North landmarks include the **North Brothers state historical marker**, which is across from the Chamber of Commerce offices (753 33rd Avenue) and **Frank North's home**, still a private residence, at 2004 15th Street.

Driving west on 11th Street to its intersection with 23rd Avenue, you'll arrive at the saloon where Buffalo Bill supposedly (but highly unlikely) paid for drinks with a g-note. Today known as **Glur's Tavern** (2301 11th Street), this bar has never

Frank North's Columbus home.

The 1876 Bucher's Saloon, now known as Glur's Tavern, stands as the oldest continually operating saloon in one location west of the Missouri.

closed or moved since its opening in 1876 as Bucher's Saloon. Louis Glur (pronounced *GLOO-er*) was hired as a teenage employee in 1903 and, a decade later, bought the place and changed the name. The Glur family sold out in 1977, but the place retains their name.

That longevity makes Glur's the oldest continually operating tavern west of the Missouri River still in its original building and location (in case you're wondering, they offered root beer and playing cards during Prohibition). In 1975, it was named to the National Register of Historic Places. The exterior looks much the same as it did in Buffalo Bill's time, and the interior has sort of an Old West sports-bar theme, serving beer, burgers, fries, and other bar fare.

A final Buffalo Bill stop is the twenty-eight-room **home of Dr. C. D. Evans** (2204 14th Street), where Cody was entertained during his 1912 and 1914 visits by his friends (the doctor's wife was Frank North's niece). This is a spectacular home, combining architectural styles of Renaissance, Greek, and Spanish Colonial—the Union Pacific ran a spur up the house to deliver its four massive columns during construction from 1908 to 1911. No tours are offered as the home is now professional offices.

On to Omaha

An 1872 visit to Omaha by Buffalo Bill Cody included friends and
fellow performers. From left: Elisha Green, Texas Jack Omohundro,
a Mr. Scott (a hatter from Chicago), Cody, and Eugene Overton.

Omaha, Nebraska, was a primary "gateway to the West" in the time of Buffalo Bill. As the head of the track and the headquarters for the Union Pacific Railroad, the majority of travelers to and from the West Coast passed through the city.

Omaha was well known to Cody—probably the reason he made the city his launch for the show. His first visit was likely in 1870. The November 13 Omaha *Daily Herald* made special note:

> Buffalo Bill is in town. Our readers are, no doubt, familiar with some of the exploits of this famous scout and guide. One of our reporters interviewed the gentleman yesterday and found him a modest, quiet man. His real name is William Cody. He was born in Davenport, Ia., and is 34 [actually 24]. He has been on the plains 27 years and for the last seven has been an army scout. He is a strongly built man, 6 feet 1 inch, and rather good looking. . . . Although Buffalo Bill is able to "hoe his own row" on the plains, he feels rather strange in a city, and consequently has engaged a guide to "take him around" while he remains in Omaha.

Cody stopped in the city again in January 1872 following the Royal Buffalo Hunt with Grand Duke Alexis. While transferring a buffalo head and hides from the hunt to Professor Henry Ward for taxidermy, he stopped at the studios of Edric Eaton for a photograph of himself to include in Alexis's photos.

He was again in Omaha just a few months later while returning to Fort McPherson from Chicago and New York, staying at the luxurious Paxton Hotel. Still later in 1872, he was in the city with his family, but they went on to St. Louis while he remained here with Texas Jack Omonduro and was entertained by friends for a day or two. He also performed in Omaha with the Buffalo Bill Combination at least twice in the years leading up to his new presentation on the Wild West.

An inaugural performance within the friendly confines of Omaha was in order. The grounds of the Omaha Driving Park on the north side of town were reserved for the production company and the anticipated crowd of eight thousand. Huge advertisements were placed on the front page of the Omaha *Daily Herald*, proclaiming the "Stupendous Inauguration of Buffalo Bill and Dr. Carver's Heroic, Vivid, Realistic and Thrilling Pictures from the Plains."

The production was much anticipated, with the newspapers reporting the unloading and transportation of the people, animals, and equipment.

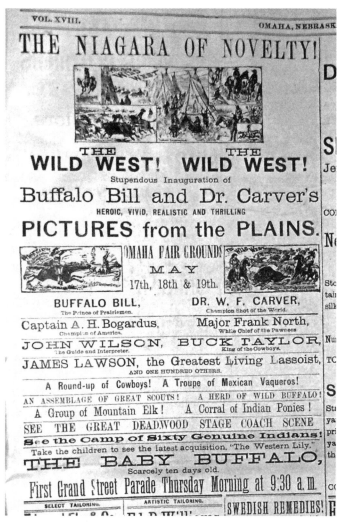

Advertisement for the first performance of the "Wild West," from the Omaha Herald.

The Omaha *Bee* noted: "The party comprises about eighty men and more than that number of animals. There are over sixty Indians—Omahas, Oglala Sioux, Brule Sioux and Pawnees. Then there are buffalos, elk, dogs, and about fifty broncho ponies. Altogether the personnel of the party is very moral and the appearance well calculated to attract attention."

Rain delayed the inaugural performance for two days. The clouds finally broke on Saturday, May 19, and nearly eight thousand were in attendance to witness history. The opening parade began with a twenty-piece marching band, followed by "Little Sitting Bull" on his pony; three Pawnees on ponies; three grown buffalo and a calf; Omaha Indian families on ponies; around forty Sioux and Pawnee braves on horseback; Cody and Carver (to wild cheers); a party of cowboys; two strings of elk; a pair of burros with packs, a dog team, and a goat team driven by Indian boys; the Deadwood stagecoach; and finally another band.

The performances were called by "Pop" Whiteker, a well-known athletic event announcer from New York, and included Indian races on horseback, a Pony Express demonstration, and an attack on the stagecoach by the Indians thwarted at the last minute by Cody and Carver and their scouts. There were shooting demonstrations by the two alongside Captain Adam Bogardus. The finale was a buffalo charge that had the animals seem to head straight for the audience until the cowboys turned them back at the last second.

To conclude the production, Cody gave a speech in which he said he trusted the enterprise had pleased the people and that he had aimed to make it "a thoroughbred Nebraska show" in which they should "hold the mirror up to nature." Thunderous applause followed. For the next thirty years, Cody would add the title of "showman" to his resume.

Omaha's Paxton Hotel in the 1880s, Cody's preferred hotel when visiting the city.

Omaha adopted Cody. Even when he wasn't in Omaha on tour or personal business, the newspapers wrote of Buffalo Bill for its readers. One story in the *Herald* was a letter from England in February 1888 in which Cody pined for Nebraska and wide-open spaces. "I want to come home," he wrote. "We are doing an immense business here, but the country cramps me and the climate chokes me. There is not air enough. If I start out to take a ride on my horse just as soon as I get warm in my saddle I've come to the end of the island. If I get comfortably fixed in their d— railway coaches the guard announces that we've arrived."

He was back in Omaha at the end of that tour in November 1888 with plans to return to the Scout's Rest Ranch. "I have determined," said Cody in an interview, "to go home and be introduced to my friends, and especially my family, at North Platte. I have not been there for two years and am anxious to get acquainted." Before that, he said, he would take a drive around Omaha to see its improvements from the previous two years.

The generosity of Cody was reported in the local papers as well. "The Hon. Bison William Cody, who has been in and about the city for the past two weeks," wrote the *Herald* on January 11, 1889, "has left several mementoes with his friends as keepsakes and proofs of his friendship." The paper went on to list six friends receiving jewelry from him and the respective values, ranging from five hundred to fifteen hundred dollars. "[He] will be at the Paxton [Hotel] on Sunday morning and distribute to any friends who may call the remainder of his collection of diamonds." It can be expected that more than a few people who had merely seen Cody in previous years "reacquainted" themselves with him and his generosity.

Grand Court of the Trans-Mississippi Exposition.

A newspaper advertisement for "Cody Day" at the Trans-Mississippi Exposition.

Buffalo Bill's Wild West and its other manifestations were presented in Omaha a dozen times, but by far the biggest offering occurred during the 1898 Trans-Mississippi Exposition and Indian Congress, the city's version of a world's fair.

August 31 was proclaimed "Cody Day" by the city of Omaha to honor the state's favorite son. One of Nebraska's U.S. senators, the sitting governor, and four former governors were present for the day's events, along with twenty-four thousand people, while another thirteen thousand came to pay their respects that evening. Waves of cheers greeted Cody as he entered the arena and took his seat with the dignitaries.

Among the speakers was Alexander Majors, Cody's old employer from Leavenworth and Russell, Majors and Waddell, who told of paying the young Cody in half dollars that the boy tied up in a handkerchief and spread out on a table before his mother. "And I have been spreading it ever since," Cody interrupted to laughter. Ever the promoter, Cody tried to meet with the Apache chief Geronimo at the expo to convince him to join his Wild West, but the chief declined.

Cody brought his show to Omaha eight more times after the Trans-Mississippi Expo and visited on countless other occasions. After Cody's death in 1917, considerable efforts were made to create a museum to him in Omaha. Dexter Fellows, an advance agent for the Ringling Bros. and Barnum & Bailey Circus and a twelve-year associate of Buffalo Bill, said both Omaha and Cody, Wyoming, were logical locations for such a memorial. "Omaha was the playground of Buffalo Bill," Fellows said in 1926. "It was here that he always came to have his fun after the hard rounds of the show." Unfortunately, the plans never materialized.

AMUSEMENTS.

Last Day - Today

Wednesday, Aug. 31,

.....ALSO.....

Cody Day-Today

AT THE EXPOSITION.

Grand Parade and Review

At 11 o'clock this Forenoon, at the Exposition, led by Col. W. F. Cody (Buffalo Bill), and reviewed by the Authorities.

An Exchange of Greetings upon the Midway, as

Buffalo Bill's Wild West

Has been the one supreme attraction at every exposition held in Europe and America during the past fifteen years with but one unimportant exception.

Regular Exhibitions this Afternoon and Evening at the Grounds at

Twentieth and Paul Streets

RAIN OR SHINE.

Seats on sale at Kuhn & Co.'s drug store, corner 15th and Douglas streets. ADMISSION—50c; children under 9, 25c; reserved seats, $1.00.

The Trail Today

Omaha has a rather notorious reputation for tearing down its history, so one tends to find sites and markers rather than actual historic structures in the city today.

The Omaha Driving Park, site of the **first performance of Cody and Carver's show**, was at the intersection of 18th and Sprague Streets. Homes now cover the site, but a historical marker commemorating both that show and Cody's historic presentation at the 1898 Trans-Mississippi Exposition is located at nearby Kountz Park at the northeast corner of Florence Boulevard and Pinkney Street. The Trans-Mississippi show was about two miles south of the park, near 20th and Paul Streets.

The **Paxton Hotel**, where Buffalo Bill was a regular guest and had his "great diamond giveaway," was demolished in 1927 and replaced by a second Paxton Hotel the following year. That Art Deco structure still stands today at 1403 Farnam Street, where it has been converted into luxury condominiums.

Buffalo Bill's Wild West

Cabinet card for Cody from "Buffalo Bill's Wild West."

As popular as the Cody–Carver production proved to be in Omaha and its other American dates, it was destined not to continue. The two simply did not get along. Both were drinkers—Carver a belligerent one who once smashed a rifle over his horse's head and struck an assistant. Cody was the one popular with the press, too, since he was the authentic Westerner while Carver simply pretended to be one.

Hastening the split was Nate Salsbury, an actor-manager-promoter who had earlier discussed a Wild West–type show with Cody when neither had the money to launch one. Now both had cash, and neither wanted Carver in the picture. The tipping point for Cody came when Carver proposed a winter tour, which Cody opposed. They closed their season in Omaha and split their assets with the flip of a coin, with Cody getting the Deadwood stagecoach.

Under the new name of "Buffalo Bill's Wild West," the show made its first appearance in St. Louis in May 1884, and for the next few years, it traveled extensively throughout the eastern states and Canada, with extended stays in major cities. The 1886 tour, for example, included a winter season at Madison Square Garden in New York City from Thanksgiving through Washington's Birthday 1887.

Buffalo Bill's production featured performances by real cowboys, real Indians, real animals, and a real stagecoach from the West. The stories told weren't always real, but that wasn't the point—they *became* real to the audience. The myths became facts to the people of the East Coast and came to represent all of America to the show patrons in Europe.

Buffalo Bill Cody with Indians of the Wild West.

The Cavalry Maze, in which riders from different countries took part in the Wild West's arena.

Cody and his crew were changing perceptions about the West. Cowboys were previously thought to be wild, armed desperadoes. President Chester A. Arthur called them "menaces to the peace of Arizona Territory" in 1881. In Buffalo Bill's portrayal, they became strong, friendly, and quite often handsome guardians of the trail. In fact, he made stars out of them. Buck Taylor, who learned the cowboy trade at Cody's ranch in Nebraska, became "King of the Cowboys." Cody's foster son, Johnny Baker, became "the Cowboy Kid." Even Sitting Bull, who had earned the fear and hatred of the nation for the defeat of Custer at Little Bighorn, gained fame and a small fortune traveling with Buffalo Bill for part of a season, although he gave much of the money away.

Sitting Bull agreed to tour with Cody only because of the chance it offered him to see the young lady he called "Little Sure Shot" on a daily basis. Annie Oakley was by far the biggest star of Buffalo Bill's Wild West. Her incredible sharpshooting and trick-shooting skills kept audiences entertained and for more than fifteen years drew people to the exhibition to see her split playing cards, shoot apples from the mouths of poodles, and shoot targets behind her using a mirror to aim.

The first overseas trip of the Wild West took place in March 1887 aboard the steamship *State of Nebraska.* Many of the Indians, having never before traveled on a ship, let alone seen an ocean, feared for their lives upon boarding but were pleased to arrive intact in England, where the production became the featured attraction in London at the American Exposition organized for Queen Victoria's Golden Jubilee. Twenty to forty thousand

Annie Oakley.

The steamship State of Nebraska *and its passenger list for the first transatlantic trip made by Buffalo Bill's Wild West. The steamer had been in service for seven years and was likely specified by Cody for the historical voyage.*

PASSENGER LIST
BUFFALO BILL'S WILD WEST SHOW,
PER STEAMER "STATE OF NEBRASKA," P. G. BRAES, Commander.
FOR LONDON DIRECT, MARCH 31st, 1887.

attended each performance during its five months at Earl's Court. Cody and his performers were welcomed into British society, with Cody himself meeting Oscar Wilde and the parents of a young Winston Churchill and visiting Parliament. Special performances were given for the Prince and Princess of Wales, as well as for Queen Victoria, making it the first time since the death of her consort Prince Albert that she had attended a public entertainment. She also stood and bowed before the American flag—unprecedented for an English monarch. The patriotic Cody was exceedingly proud.

The pinnacle of Buffalo Bill's Wild West (with the added Congress of Rough Riders of the World) came with the World's Columbian Exposition in Chicago in 1893. Cody wanted to be on the fair's midway, but the organizers rejected the request. Instead, he and his partners bought land near the expo's entrance and started operating the show to daily sellouts of eighteen thousand people a month before the expo opened. They were open on Sunday when the fair was closed. They even gave free admission and food to the poor children of the city when the expo's officials backed out on a promise to them—and the newspapers and people of Chicago loved Buffalo Bill all the more. By the end of their stay, Buffalo Bill's Wild West had entertained more than four million people.

In 1895, the new Wild West had a new partner, James Bailey of Barnum & Bailey Circus fame. Bailey brought funds and a new way of presenting by taking a schedule similar to a circus. In visiting more cities in shorter runs—setting up the tents for a day instead of weeks—Buffalo Bill was now

Running the Wild West

In the course of putting on one of the world's first and most successful traveling exhibitions, Cody had several persons essential to its success and continuity.

Although partners, joint proprietors, and co-creators of the production, Cody and Nate Salsbury couldn't have been more different. Cody was the free-spending public figure and Salsbury was the sharp business manager behind the scenes who was missed greatly when he died in 1902.

Salsbury had a strong personal influence over Cody. In the early days of the production, Cody allowed many of his old friends to join him in getting drunk, entirely at his expense. Salsbury dropped the hammer on Cody and his behavior, causing Cody to swear to never be drunk in front of Salsbury as long as they were in partnership. It was a promise he kept reasonably well.

John Burke was called "Major" in spite of never serving in the military; he also called himself "Arizona John" when on stage, even though he'd never traveled west of the Mississippi before meeting Cody. One thing that wasn't a lie was that he was a master of publicity for his boss for nearly thirty-five years.

Burke seemingly knew every editor at every newspaper in every town, and was particularly talented at getting them to write glowing words about Buffalo Bill and his show. He'd send in crews weeks before performances to post large, colorful posters throughout the town to promote Buffalo Bill's Wild West. By the time it arrived, people practically stampeded to the ticket stand. Burke created many of the legends of Buffalo Bill, which means he also bears some

Nate Salsbury.

Maj. John Burke.

expanding into the Great Plains, bringing the show to towns like Council Bluffs, Wichita, Sioux Falls, and Lincoln. The travel schedule brought Buffalo Bill and his performers to many more people. It was very profitable, but it was also exhausting—in 1896, the route covered 10,000 miles with 132 stops.

By the end of the century, the show itself was becoming a little tired— and stale—as well. Attendance was falling off as people knew what to expect. Economic downturns hurt it, too. The partnership had the idea to go back to Europe in 1902 since it hadn't been there for a decade. The

responsibility for the decline of Cody's reputation when those legends stretched the truth.

Johnny Baker was a boy who lived on the ranch next to Cody's at North Platte. Thrilled to have the legend living next door, Baker began his career by tagging along after Cody, holding his horse as the legend made stops around town. Cody took a liking to the little hero-worshipper, who at nine in 1878 was about the same age as his son Kit would have been. As the boy grew and Cody gave him more tasks, Baker became his foster son. He became skilled in frontier ways and even a performer in his idol's show.

Johnny Baker.

Baker was an expert marksman in the show as "the Cowboy Kid," talented enough to become one of its headliners. After Nate Salsbury died, Baker started taking on more responsibility in managing the show. Buffalo Bill himself said, "No father ever had a son more loving and faithful. You have done as much to make the Wild West what it is as I have myself."

Barnum & Bailey Circus would tour America at the same time, and thus, the productions wouldn't compete.

Before the show opened in London, Nate Salsbury died on Christmas Eve 1902 after a lingering illness. This was a tremendous blow to the show and to Cody, who had even more personal losses ahead of him. His daughter Arta died two years later. He went through the divorce trial against Louisa in 1905. James Bailey died in 1906, after which Bailey's estate demanded payment of his share of the show.

A series of bad investments also took its toll on Cody and the production. Touring continued in Europe, but financial help was needed with the return to America. The "white knight" came in the form of former employee and present competitor Gordon Lillie. Lillie, performing under the name of "Pawnee Bill," had a traveling show that emphasized the Far East instead of the Wild West. As both were seeing declines in business, Cody and Lillie decided to merge their shows. Buffalo Bill's Wild West and Pawnee Bill's Far East began in 1909.

Cody was sixty-four years old in 1910 and decided it would be a good time to retire. He announced it at Madison Square Garden and began a two-year farewell tour. The shows initially were great moneymakers, but as Cody continued to put his profits into bad investments and show profits decreased in 1911 due to bad weather and a poor economy, he found that he couldn't afford to retire. He continued into 1912 without mentioning his retirement.

He sold his Scout's Rest Ranch to Lillie and also mortgaged the Irma Hotel in Wyoming to him. It paid off some of his debt to Lillie, but Cody still needed cash to keep the show on the road—which, unfortunately, he mentioned to Harry Tammen while visiting Denver.

Tammen owned the *Denver Post* and the Sells-Floto Circus, a small circus that its owner wanted to move into the big time. He was more than happy to loan Cody the amount he wanted and, once the loan was signed, made the announcement that Buffalo Bill's Wild West would separate from Pawnee Bill's Far East in 1914. Cody either didn't read the terms or didn't understand them, but he was convinced he hadn't agreed to a separation from Pawnee Bill and told Lillie to ignore the announcement. Lillie believed Cody was leaving their partnership, however, and left Cody to deal with his financial problems on his own. During their last year together, 1913, their show stopped in Denver at the same time the note was due, and when they were unable to pay, a sheriff's sale was held. Ultimately, Lillie was able to save his wealth but was never able to get back into show business.

Worse for Cody, he now was working for Tammen. The Sells-Floto Circus and Buffalo Bill's Wild West were combined for 1914, but Cody was about all that remained to do the show. For his part, Cody did local promotion and interviews and introduced the show from his saddle, but he did no shooting or other performances. He signed on for an additional year, hoping to raise enough money to start his own show again. In 1916, before Cody could start another production, Tammen claimed that *he* now owned the name "Buffalo Bill" and Cody would have to pay him five thousand dollars to reclaim it. Cody grudgingly paid.

Cody wasn't in shape to start his own show again, physically or financially. He began touring with the 101 Ranch in Oklahoma, one of the few

Wild West shows still in the business. He was happy with the company, where he was among cowboys and Indians and Johnny Baker once again.

More than thirty years had passed since Cody opened in Omaha with what became Buffalo Bill's Wild West. He was now seventy and could no longer get up to or down from his saddle without Baker's help. The 1916 season closed on November 11 in Portsmouth, Virginia, and although no one knew it, it was the last public appearance of William F. "Buffalo Bill" Cody.

Related Sites

Buffalo Bill performed across the Great Plains and beyond—and may even have visited your town. The Buffalo Bill Museum at Golden, Colorado, has compiled a comprehensive listing of all of the locations where Cody is known to have performed in fourteen countries, forty-eight states and territories, and the District of Columbia. To see if his tours included your town, visit www.buffalobill.org/PDFs/Buffalo_Bill_Visits.pdf.

The roots of the 101 Ranch Wild West Show lie with the 101 Ranch of Ponca City, Oklahoma. The Miller brothers, who owned the 110,000-acre cattle ranch, decided to get into the circus business on the recommendation of their neighbor, Gordon "Pawnee Bill" Lillie. They were late getting into the business in 1907, however, and suffered from the growing popularity of motion pictures. They also had a string of bad luck: a train wreck killed many of the show's animals, several cast members contracted typhoid fever, and some of their Indians were taken by the German government in World War I under suspicion of being Serbian spies (and were never seen again). After Cody's death, the Millers' show limped along at a much smaller scale before finally closing for good after the 1939 New York World's Fair, following the 101 Ranch's bankruptcy in 1932. The site of the ranch is a national historic landmark, with an historical marker thirteen miles southwest of Ponca City on Oklahoma Highway 156 (the 101 Ranch Memorial Road). There's also a mural that celebrates the 101 Ranch and Wild West Show at 207 West Grand Avenue in Ponca City.

Recommended Reading

Buffalo Bill: Scout, Showman, Visionary by Steve Friesen (Golden, CO: Fulcrum Books, 2010); *Annie Oakley of the Wild West* by Walter Havighurst (New York: Macmillan, 1954. Reprint, Lincoln: University of Nebraska Press, 1992); *The Colonel and Little Missie: Buffalo Bill, Annie Oakley, and the Beginnings of Superstardom in America* by Larry McMurtry (New York: Simon & Schuster, 2005); *Buffalo Bill's America: William Cody and the Wild West Show* by Louis S. Warren (New York: Knopf, 2005).

Fort Yates
and the Rescue
of Sitting Bull

Cabinet card of Sitting Bull and Buffalo Bill in 1885.

Cody was in Europe in 1890 with the Wild West, but problems were developing at home to pull him back to America. Rumors were circulating that he had mistreated the Indians in the show, and although the Bureau of Indian Affairs was satisfied they were well fed, well paid, and happy, stories continued to appear in the eastern press. And back in Nebraska, an argument began between Louisa and Bill's sister Julia over the management of the Scout's Rest Ranch.

The Wild West was put into winter camp in Alsace-Lorraine, with Cody, Major Burke, and the agency Indians returning stateside to testify to their treatment. Just as his ship arrived in New York, Cody was handed a telegram: Gen. Nelson A. Miles wanted him at Fort Yates in the Dakota Territory to bring in Sitting Bull.

Fort Yates last figured prominently in Old West history when Sitting Bull returned to the Standing Rock Agency from imprisonment at Fort Randall in 1883. He then traveled with showman Alvaren Allen in late 1884 and with Buffalo Bill Cody's Wild West Show the following year. He declined to continue with the show in 1887, choosing to stay at Standing Rock and fight attempts to buy out the Sioux land. The assignment for the retired scout came about because of a potentially explosive situation with the Ghost Dance craze that year. A Paiute shaman named Wovoka (or Jack Wilson) brought a new religion to the Indian peoples incorporating elements of Christianity and traditional Indian beliefs. A main element of the craze was that if prescribed rituals were followed, the ancestors of the adherents would rise from the dead and the believers would reclaim the land lost to whites while living in peace among them.

From his Grand River cabin on the Standing Rock Reservation, Sitting Bull was not among its followers, but was intrigued by it. Some suggest that the Hunkpapa chief may have seen the religion as an opportunity to regain some of the stature he had lost in recent years.

Many of the Indian agents feared the movement, including the Standing Rock agent James McLaughlin, who neither liked nor trusted Sitting Bull and expected the chief to use the movement as an opportunity to stir dissent on the reservation. When Sitting Bull asked to visit the Pine Ridge Agency, where Wovoka was expected to visit, McLaughlin turned him down.

When it was determined that the safest course of action was to have Sitting Bull at the fort, General Miles wrote to Cody, authorizing him to go to Sitting Bull's cabin on the reservation and bring him in. As Cody wrote in his autobiography:

Miles said that Sitting Bull had his camp somewhere within forty or fifty miles of the Standing Rock Agency, and was haranguing the Indians thereabout, spreading the Messiah talk and getting them to join him. He asked me if I could go immediately to Standing Rock and Fort Yates, and thence to Sitting Bull's camp. He knew that I was an old friend of the chief and he believed that if any one could induce the old fox to abandon his place for a general war I could. . . . I was sure that if I could reach Sitting Bull he would at least listen to me.

Cody arrived at the Standing Rock Agency and Fort Yates on November 28, 1890, to carry out Miles's request. Miles saw it as an arrest, Cody apparently viewed it as an attempt to take Sitting Bull in, and McLaughlin foresaw a potential disaster with bloodshed likely. He planned to arrest Sitting Bull on ration day when most of the other Indians were at the agency and the chief would be alone at his cabin.

McLaughlin wired the Commissioner of Indian Affairs, advising against Cody's trip and asking the commissioner to intercept the order. In the meantime, officers at the adjacent Fort Yates (according to popular accounts) tried to delay Cody by getting him drunk. They apparently didn't know of Buffalo Bill's reputation; he easily out-drank anyone at the officers' club who challenged him.

Fort Yates in the late 1870s or early 1880s, before Cody's visit.

Undaunted, Cody left as planned the next day with friends who knew Sitting Bull from his show. There was no hurry; they stopped to visit others along the route. McLaughlin, meanwhile, got word from no less an authority than President Benjamin Harrison that Cody was not to interfere. McLaughlin sent out riders to intercept Cody, who had already been told that Sitting Bull was on his way to the agency on a different road. Cody went to that road but didn't find the chief there or at the agency; he left immediately for North Platte upon his return. Sitting Bull was told that Cody was at the agency and wanted to see him, but the chief refused to go there and thus sealed his doom.

The agent convinced the commander of Fort Yates to let him execute the arrest of Sitting Bull using the U.S. Indian Police—native Sioux who answered to McLaughlin. This would minimize the chance of bloodshed, McLaughlin said, and he ordered Sitting Bull's arrest, sending forty-three Indian Police to carry out the order while two troops of the Eighth Cavalry stood by several miles away. One hour before dawn on December 15, they arrested Sitting Bull in his cabin without incident. Once they began treating him roughly, however, he resisted as friends began to gather around. One of them shot Lieutenant Bull Head, the officer in charge, who in turn fired at Sitting Bull. Another officer, Sergeant Red Tomahawk, also fired on Sitting Bull. Either shot might have killed him.

A furious gunfight broke out, and the policemen sought cover in the cabin. While the shooting went on, Sitting Bull's gray horse (given to him by Buffalo Bill) began performing tricks as he'd been trained to do in the Wild West show. He sat down as bullets flew by, raising a hoof. The action terrified the Indian Police, who thought Sitting Bull's spirit had entered the horse. (The horse was unhurt, and Cody later took him back as a standard bearer for the Wild West at the Columbian Exposition.)

By the time the fight was over, four Indian Police were dead and two, including Bull Head, were mortally wounded. Eight of Sitting Bull's followers were dead in addition to their chief. The remaining Indians scattered when the cavalry came up, allowing the surviving Indian Police to retreat with their dead and Sitting Bull's body. Put in a homemade coffin filled with quicklime, Sitting Bull was buried in a corner of the Fort Yates military cemetery.

The Trail Today

The majority of troops abandoned **Fort Yates** in 1895, and the last caretaker troops left in 1903. The town of Fort Yates, which sprung up around the post and Standing Rock Agency, remains today as the Hunkpapa Sioux tribal headquarters. The only building that remains from the military post is the 1870s-era guardhouse, located at the southeast corner of Cottonwood Street and Proposal Avenue. Buffalo Bill would have seen the two-story wood-frame building while here. Tribal stories say Sitting Bull was once a prisoner, although no documentation has been found. It is now owned by the Bureau of Indian Affairs, which is transferring ownership of the building to the Standing Rock Tribe for an art gallery.

Sitting Bull's gravesite is in view of the building on Yates Street (the only road into town) near its intersection with Dike Street. In 1953, businessmen from Mobridge, South Dakota, aided by Sitting Bull's descendants, dug up the grave in the dark of night, retrieved some bones, and buried them on a bluff overlooking the Missouri River near Mobridge, adding tons of concrete and steel on top for good measure. Later studies by the State Historical Society of North Dakota at the Fort Yates site reported most or all of Sitting Bull's bones were still there. In 2007 the state gave the burial site to the Standing Rock Tribe, which improved and restored the site with interpretive markers.

The South Dakota burial site for Sitting Bull is about fifty-eight miles south on Highway 1806, four miles south of the junction of 1806 and U.S. 12. His grave is topped with a massive granite bust sculpture by Korczak Ziolkowski, whose family is now carving the Crazy Horse Memorial in the Black Hills.

North of the gravesite, and west of the intersection of Proposal Avenue and Church Street, is a Catholic cemetery and the **U.S. Indian Police**

The Fort Yates guardhouse today.

Sitting Bull's gravesite at Fort Yates. NORTH DAKOTA PARKS AND RECREATION

gravesite. The six policemen killed during Sitting Bull's arrest are buried here together—look for the large reddish marker.

Related Site

Cody never made it to **Sitting Bull's cabin** on the Grand River, and not many do today. There is a South Dakota state historical marker at the location, but it is in a very remote area at the end of a ten-mile dirt road that is possible to travel only in the best of conditions. On top of that, mountain lions have been known to frequent the area. Local tribe members prefer to keep the road as is to discourage tourism.

The author attempted a visit but was turned back by muddy road conditions and cannot recommend it. Should the reader attempt the trip, start from the town of McLaughlin (named for the agent), South Dakota, twenty-eight miles northwest of Mobridge on U.S. 12. Take Highway 63 south for nearly four miles and turn west on 113th Street/Bullhead Road. After nine miles you'll reach an unmarked dirt road headed south—this is the ten-mile road to the Grand River and the marker for Sitting Bull's cabin. Good luck.

Recommended Reading

The Saga of Sitting Bull's Bones by Robb DeWall (Crazy Horse, SD: Korczak's Heritage, Inc., 1984); *The Lance and the Shield: The Life and Times of Sitting Bull* by Robert M. Utley (New York: Henry Holt, 1993).

Wounded Knee

Cody and Miles viewing the Indian camp near Pine Ridge, South Dakota, on January 16, 1891.

Because of the killing of Sitting Bull on the Grand River, many of his followers fled south to join the Miniconjous on the Cheyenne River Reservation. Those people were already preparing to come into the Pine Ridge Agency as requested, but the news from the north had them in a panic, fearing similar treachery. The situation was made worse when military forces, including the Seventh Cavalry, intercepted the Indians.

The troops surrounded the band of Indians at Wounded Knee Creek on December 29, 1890, and began to enforce an order to surrender arms. Some of the Indians balked at the order, and a shot was fired. Gunfire broke out and a melee became a massacre, with about three hundred Lakota killed, two-thirds of whom were women and children. Thirty-one soldiers were killed, with some of the military deaths the result of friendly fire.

Cody was in North Platte after his mission to bring in Sitting Bull failed. He came to Wounded Knee after the massacre, sent by Nebraska governor John Thayer to join the Nebraska National Guard. The governor suggested that Cody's "superior knowledge of Indian character and mode of warfare" might be of value to Gen. L. W. Colby, the commander of the Nebraska National Guard. The governor felt that Cody's presence as an officer, former scout, and citizen of nearby Nebraska would have a calming influence on the settlers there.

Cody arrived at Pine Ridge and Wounded Knee on January 9, 1891, to find the site covered with newspaper correspondents and troops. If Cody calmed the settlers to the south in Nebraska, he had the same effect on the soldiers on the field: "It certainly impressed us very much to see what influence 'Buffalo Bill' had over several thousand bloodthirsty redskins," wrote William J. Slaughter, a former trooper with the Seventh Cavalry.

Major Burke was already there with around fifty Indians from the Wild West show employed as Indian Police. The Indian agent at Pine Ridge interviewed those Indians, who confirmed that they were very happy with Cody and with their pay, food, clothing, and general welfare.

General Miles announced the end of the campaign on January 11 and formally advised General Colby that the Nebraska troops could be withdrawn. The Indians formally surrendered on January 16, turning over nineteen of their leaders (who soon joined Buffalo Bill's Wild West in Europe as performers).

Cody reviewed the troops with Miles and other officers and then departed to visit towns in northern Nebraska along the Fremont, Elkhorn, & Missouri Valley Railroad to calm the fears of settlers. With the Indians having surrendered and the press now satisfied by Cody's treatment of

Cody and Maj. John Burke (seated, front at right) at Pine Ridge Reservation with Indian performers from the Wild West show.

them in his show, Buffalo Bill's involvement in the Indian wars was now limited to its presentation.

This was not his final trip to Pine Ridge, however. In 1913, with the support of the Secretary of War and the Department of the Interior, Cody stepped into the burgeoning film business to create historical films. He brought together six hundred troopers of the Twentieth Cavalry and agency Indians to recreate battles of the Indian wars for film. General Miles and other retired commanders appeared, along with Indian chiefs who had been in Cody's Wild West. One of the films was shot at Wounded Knee, with survivors of the fight and those with family members killed there. It was rumored that some young warriors planned vengeance by putting live ammunition in their guns, but tribal elders interceded to assure the filming was completed safely.

The Trail Today

The **Wounded Knee massacre site** is located on the Pine Ridge Reservation, eighteen miles northeast of the town of Pine Ridge via U.S. 18 and BIA 27. The site is scarred by the highway's route right through its middle.

A large marker at a pull-off tells the story of the massacre, a portion of which occurred in the fields and ravines around you. Immediately visible

From "Honorable" to "Colonel" to "General" W. F. Cody

In 1887, Nebraska governor John Thayer appointed and commissioned William F. Cody as aide-de-camp of his staff with the rank of colonel in the Nebraska National Guard. This honorary but largely meaningless title was fully embraced by Cody and by Maj. John Burke, who immediately replaced "Hon(orable)" with "Col." in promoting Cody and their show, especially overseas.

Burke took it even further, drawing on Cody's scouting days. Cody was now "Col. W. F. Cody, Chief of Scouts, U.S. Army." Of course, he was only the chief of scouts of one regiment of cavalry rather than the entire army, and he was not a colonel in the army.

While in South Dakota following the massacre at Wounded Knee, a pre-Wounded Knee designation from Governor Thayer went into effect: "Colonel" Cody became "General" Cody.

Thayer ordered Cody to meet with General Miles there on "special service" (which was never disclosed) and, if time allowed, to visit the towns along the northern tier of Nebraska to calm any fears those residents had. The governor suggested that Cody's "superior knowledge of Indian character and mode of warfare" might be of value to Gen. L. W. Colby, commander of the Nebraska National Guard.

It appears Cody wasn't that fond of the title "general." He used it in an introduction to a book by his old boss, Alexander Majors, and a couple of other publications, but it wasn't splashed around like "Col. W. F. Cody."

Russell reports a story of an Indian friend asking him if he was now General Cody instead of Colonel Cody. When Cody said yes, the Indian further asked, "You big general same as General Brooke and General Miles?"

"Well, not exactly," Cody said. "My commission is in the Nebraska National Guard."

"Milish (militia)—oh hell," said the Indian with a snort.

In 1895, Nebraska governor Silas Holcomb recommissioned Cody as a colonel, probably at Cody's insistence.

Cody in uniform as colonel in the Nebraska National Guard.

The memorial to those slain at Wounded Knee stands before the mass grave and overlooks the massacre site in the background.

Red Cloud's grave, north of Pine Ridge, South Dakota.

to the northwest is a hill with a cemetery—it was here that the Hotchkiss guns were trained on the people during the massacre. At the center of the small cemetery is a fenced enclosure holding the mass grave of those killed in 1890 as well as a monument to Chief Big Foot and others.

This is one of the poorest areas in the nation. Depending upon when you visit the site, you may be approached by Lakota asking you to purchase trinkets to help fight alcoholism and drug use among their youth. It's probably good karma to do so.

Related Site

The **grave of Red Cloud** is not far from here. Four miles north of Pine Ridge on U.S. 18 is the Red Cloud Indian School, formerly the Holy Rosary Mission and, before that, the Drexel Mission.

Parking near the old mission building, you'll notice a large marker with the story of the great chief next to a road going up a small hill. The cemetery is at the top, with Red Cloud's grave toward the back and right within the fenced enclosure.

To the right of Red Cloud's grave is that of a headliner in Buffalo Bill's Wild West, William "Bronco Bill" Irving.

Recommended Reading

Eyewitness at Wounded Knee by Richard E. Jensen, et al. (Lincoln: University of Nebraska Press, 1991).

Buffalo Bill Goes to Wyoming

William F. Cody in the 1890s.
KANSAS HISTORICAL SOCIETY

Buffalo Bill Cody grew increasingly interested in moving to Wyoming in the mid-1890s, specifically to the Bighorn Mountains and the adjoining Bighorn Basin.

He didn't lack reasons. For one, he had some familiarity with the area, having passed through the region during the 1870s as a scout with Generals Mills and Crook. He had heard of the richness of its soil from Professor O. C. Marsh, who searched for fossils in the basin. It held the potential for irrigation with the Shoshone River, such as he began with success in Nebraska on the North Platte River.

The move might also have had something to do with Bill Cody's innate wanderlust. He had made his home in North Platte for almost twenty years and was overdue for change. Lulu and her interest in his business and personal affairs may have made the town too crowded for him.

In 1895 Cody came to the Bighorn Basin with George T. Beck and others to supervise the construction of the Cody Canal, the first effort to irrigate the basin. He moved cattle from Nebraska and South Dakota to begin ranching along the south channel of the Shoshone. (Since the Dakota cattle already had a brand of "TE" on them, the Cody ranch was known as the TE Ranch.)

Bill and his associates staked out a new town called Cody City near the DeMaris Springs in 1895, but Beck found a better location the following year about two miles downstream on the Shoshone. The new town of Cody (dropping the "City") had streets wide enough to turn a wagon team. Bill's nephew Ed Goodman was set up as its first postmaster, and in 1899 Cody started the town's first newspaper, the *Cody Enterprise.*

Bill also was instrumental in convincing the Burlington Railroad to build a branch there in 1901. An even bigger feat of persuasion came four years later when the federal government signed on to build the first road to Yellowstone National Park out of Cody at the cost of fifty thousand dollars. President Theodore Roosevelt admitted that it was the recommendation of his old friend William F. Cody that got approval for the "Cody Road."

The house at the TE Ranch, the site of Cody's seclusion in the Rockies.

Buffalo Bill's Irma Hotel in 1903, a few months after its opening. CODY, WYOMING

"[I]f he was good enough to guide such men as Sheridan, Sherman, Carr, Custer, and Miles with their armies through uncivilized regions, I would take chances on building a road into the middle of eternity on his statement," Roosevelt said, "and Bill says it is all right, as he has been over it on horseback."

Demonstrating himself as a man ahead of his time and out of step with the present, Bill Cody in 1902 built the Irma Hotel, named for his youngest daughter. His namesake town had a little more than three hundred people, but Cody built an inn large enough for a town of several thousand. He reportedly lost five hundred dollars a month waiting for customers to fill the rooms.

Cody assumed a major role in building the new town's first church in 1902 after a high-stakes poker game. The pot with Bill and the other players got so large that they agreed that the winner should donate the winnings to their favorite church. Bill's friend George Beck won and constructed a little Episcopal church.

Also in 1902, Bill started thinking again about a divorce from Louise. He expressed a desire to live as an "honest" man and proposed giving all of the North Platte property to her in exchange for her agreement to sign the papers. Cody turned over the property, but she didn't sign and instead started getting involved in the Wyoming affairs, which led to more quarrels, especially with his sisters now living in Cody.

Their daughter Arta died in 1904. Cody took the tragic event to propose to Lulu that they forget their differences and live in peace; instead, she

Louisa and Bill Cody in his namesake town, about a year before his death.

accused Cody of breaking their daughter's heart and being the chief cause of her death. They accompanied Arta's body to Rochester for burial next to her siblings, but Lulu refused to speak to Cody and caused a scene with him and his sisters in Chicago.

The divorce hearing in Cheyenne the following year cast neither in a favorable light, with ridiculous charges by Cody that his wife attempted to poison him and by Lulu that Queen Victoria's interest in her husband had been a little too personal. Ultimately, Cody lost the divorce suit against Lulu and was compelled to pay all costs.

Cody became more religious and gave up alcohol and swearing. He also avoided Lulu and North Platte until 1910 when, while touring with the Wild

Louisa Cody with daughters Irma (left) and Arta (right) on the eve of Arta's second marriage in 1904. Arta died less than a month after the wedding due to complications from surgery.

West, he came to North Platte to visit at the request of a grandson. Lulu also happened to be there, and the offspring conspired to get them into a room together. When they emerged, all differences had apparently been patched up.

Meanwhile, with Cody's cash flow from performing still high and without Salsbury to rein in spending, activities continued in Wyoming. The irrigation project transformed into the construction of the Shoshone Dam in 1905, although the project was beyond the scope of even Buffalo Bill's wealth. He signed the rights back over to the State of Wyoming before construction.

That same year, Cody built the Wapiti Inn about a day's wagon ride from the Irma, and farther down the Cody Road, just two miles from the Yellowstone entrance, he added the Pahaska Tepee Inn and Restaurant. The plan was to cover the lodging needs of people headed to the national park—as guests of Buffalo Bill.

Simultaneously with his Wyoming investments, Cody sought to make a killing in Arizona mining. For more than a decade, starting in 1902, Cody and partners spent more than half a million dollars searching for tungsten, gold, and lead strikes that never panned out.

He spent money on other companies and products that didn't produce either. Along with that, Russell wrote, he was making thousands of loans to old scouts and out-of-luck showmen that would never be paid. His pockets were always filled with silver dollars to pass out to children who would flock around him—or to anyone who asked for one.

The free-spending started catching up with Cody. The TE Ranch, which had been expanded to more than eight thousand acres, was forced to scale back to half its size. Service was scaled back at the inns, too, as discovered by Stephen Mather, the first director of the National Park Service. During a 1916 inspection of the main route to Yellowstone National Park, he found that the Irma Hotel was anything but "the sweetest hotel that ever was," as Buffalo Bill called it.

"First of all," wrote Horace Albright, who traveled with Mather and his wife, "Mrs. Mather insisted on sitting up all night in the lobby after she discovered 'things crawling in the bed.' Mather ordered a pillow and blankets for her, saw to her comfort, and then disappeared back to the lice, bedbugs, or whatever. He didn't last long there because when he opened the door to his room he found two men asleep in his bed. Downstairs at the desk, he demanded another room. 'There is no other room,' said the clerk. 'You'll just have to make your bedfellows move over.'"

It didn't get any better when they reached the Pahaska Tepee. "It turned out to be just as bad as the Irma, if not worse," said Albright. "Lunch was one dollar, far too much for the horrible, greasy, inedible food served by loud, boisterous, grimy, but glitzy waitresses. Mather muttered to me, 'Could Cody be operating a combination eating place and brothel?' After studying the situation, he ordered us not to eat a bite. He threw cash on the table (fifty cents per person) and stalked out, vowing to make the place change or he'd close it."

In 1916, Cody was touring as much as ever to fund his lifestyle, if not his very life. He arrived in Wyoming in November after an exhausting tour season, staying at the TE Ranch for a few weeks of rest before going to his sister's home in Denver in early December. It was the last time he would see the state.

The Trail Today

Cody is a town that lives and breathes its namesake. His newspaper, the *Cody Enterprise*, is still in print. The signs, statues, and parks dedicated to Bill are everywhere and only add to the feeling of mutual love between the man and his town.

The site of the first effort at a town, the short-lived **Cody City**, is marked on the western edge of town on U.S. 14/16, east of the Cody Nite Rodeo grounds and near the Old Trail Town Museum attraction. Historical markers tell of the original town and the Indian names of the area as well as the extinct geyser basin known as Colter's Hell.

The **Cody Canal** from the Shoshone River still exists and still supplies water to the Bighorn Basin. You can cross it at several areas around town, but the story is told through displays at Canal Park, which overlooks a former section of the canal in the central part of town. You'll find a map of the original canal along with interesting bits of information. For example, the original land salesman for the canal estimated no more than 12,000 acres could be cultivated with the water. The board wanted to sell 26,000 acres, so the salesman was fired. Today the canal irrigates around 11,600 acres. The park is located north of the Park County Public Library and northeast of the Paul Stock Recreation Center, north of Stampede Avenue and east of 13th Street.

A few blocks to the northwest of the park is Cody's very first attraction for tourists, the **Irma Hotel**, at 12th Street and Sheridan Avenue. The current ownership made a substantial investment in its renovation and restoration, and one would think that William F. Cody would be proud to see it achieving the quality and popularity he had hoped for it. His private room and office are both available as suites for your stay in Cody, along with thirty-six other rooms. If you're feeling daring, request Room 35, the Irma's haunted suite. Staff and guests have all reported sighting the ghost of a Confederate officer, hearing children and a dog where there were none, watching doors rattle rapidly with no one on the other side, and feeling someone rubbing their arms.

You can also visit to refresh and restore yourself on the main floor. The Irma's famous cherrywood bar is still there and is one of the most photographed features in all of Cody. Plus, the food is *much* better than that served to the NPS director in 1916. The busy hotel restaurant is famous for its prime rib, but they also serve buffalo rib eye, "Wild West" salmon, and buffets for breakfast, lunch, and dinner. *Address:* 1192 Sheridan Avenue, Cody, Wyoming 82414. *Phone:* (307) 587-4221. *Website:* www.irmahotel.com.

Take Sheridan Avenue east from the Irma for the next must-see stop in Cody. You'll pass a statue in the city park of Buffalo Bill with a child on his shoulders and the Cody Visitor Center (built to replicate the TE Ranch house) before arriving at the **Buffalo Bill Center of the West**. Formerly

The Irma Hotel is still a popular stop for tourists in downtown Cody.

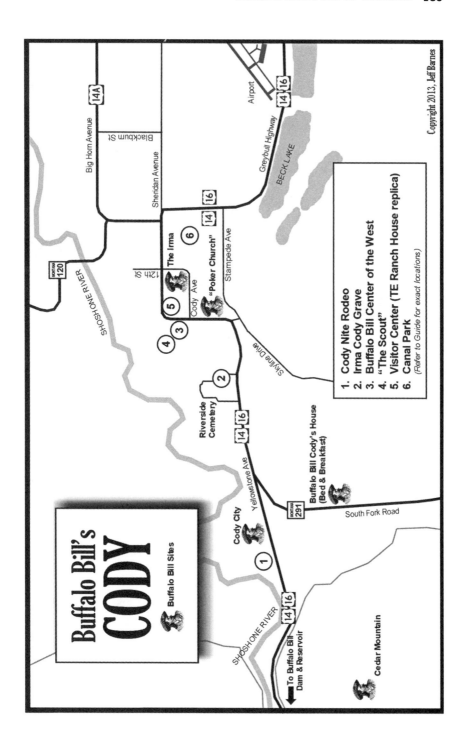

Buffalo Bill's
CODY

![Buffalo Bill Sites]

Buffalo Bill Sites

1. Cody Nite Rodeo
2. Irma Cody Grave
3. Buffalo Bill Center of the West
4. "The Scout"
5. Visitor Center (TE Ranch House replica)
6. Canal Park

(Refer to Guide for exact locations)

Copyright 2013, Jeff Barnes

A restored Deadwood-Cheyenne stagecoach at The Buffalo Bill Center of the West.

called the Buffalo Bill Historical Center, this is the top visitor attraction in Cody and for good reason. When you walk past the welcoming statue of Buffalo Bill and through the doors to pay your admission, the clerk will tell you the pass is good for two days. Don't laugh: you *will* need two days to check out everything this incredible museum has to offer.

The Buffalo Bill Center of the West is billed as five museums in one, each distinct from the other but under one roof (covering a third of a million square feet). Included are the Whitney Gallery of Western Art, an outstanding collection of paintings, sculptures, and prints from the nineteenth century through present day; the Cody Firearms Museum, with one of the world's largest and most significant collections of American and European firearms; the Plains Indian Museum, hosting one of the best collections of native art and artifacts in America; the Draper Museum of Natural History, covering the interaction of man and nature in the Greater Yellowstone ecosystem; and finally the Buffalo Bill Museum, the flagship attraction that began it all.

The museum opened in 1927 and used many of the items collected by Buffalo Bill to tell the story of his life and times. Incorporating those artifacts and more recent acquisitions, the museum was completely renovated in 2012 to make Bill more approachable to the public. In fact, Buffalo Bill "greets" *you* at the museum entrance as a friendly spirit, played by local resident Peter Simpson and rear-projected onto a screen of fine mist to welcome visitors.

Cody was the first international celebrity, and the museum tells the story of how he became that person, how he dealt with stardom, and how it affected him and those he loved. Many of the artifacts of his life help tell the story: his boyhood home; his coat as a scout; the jewelry from Grand Duke Alexis; the Deadwood stagecoach; the "Camp Monaco" painted tree stump from his last hunt; and more. All are presented unobtrusively and allow for close study. For children (of all ages), there are interactive displays and videos to further explore Buffalo Bill, while the serious student of William F. Cody will truly appreciate the McCracken Research Library. This is one of *the* great museums of the West. *Address:* 720 Sheridan Avenue, Cody, Wyoming 82414. *Hours:* Open daily from 8 A.M. to 6 P.M., May through September 15. Open daily from 10 A.M. to 5 P.M., November through April. Weekends only from December through February. Closed Thanksgiving, Christmas, and New Year's Day. *Admission:* Adults $18, seniors $16, students $14, youth (6 to 17) $10, children (5 and under) free. *Phone:* (307) 587-4771. *Website:* www.bbhc.org.

Outside, to the northwest of the museum, is the first memorial to Buffalo Bill in Cody, the massive bronze statue **"Buffalo Bill—The Scout."** The 1924 statue was commissioned by Mary Jester Allen, a niece of Buffalo Bill, to Gertrude Vanderbilt Whitney, the daughter of Cornelius Vanderbilt and a sculptor of some renown. Whitney decided to have the statue depict Cody during his frontier army days and called for a horse from the TE Ranch and a local cowboy to come to New York for modeling. Iowa, Kansas, and Nebraska were all considered as sites for the statue, but Whitney ultimately opted for Wyoming, where Cody chose to make his final home. The large stone base is meant to replicate nearby Cedar Mountain, which Cody had originally selected as his burial site (see pages 189–190), although it looks more like Rattlesnake Mountain immediately to the west.

Continuing south on U.S. 14/16 (Eighth Street), past the statue of a young Bill Cody riding in the Pony Express, make a left (east) turn onto Canyon Avenue and pull into the parking lot of the Christ Episcopal Church. Next to the garden and among the trees is the **"Poker Church,"** purchased with proceeds of the famous 1902 game with Cody, Beck, and others. This little wood-frame church hosts summer worship and special events. *Address:* 825 Simpson Avenue, Cody, Wyoming 82414. *Phone:* (307) 587-3849. *Website:* www.christchurchcody.org.

"Buffalo Bill—The Scout"

Cody's "Poker Church."

U.S. 14/16 curves to the west now as Yellowstone Avenue—keep an eye on the right for **Riverside Cemetery**. Irma Cody Garlow and her husband, Frederick Garlow, died in Cody in 1918 during the influenza epidemic of that year. (Irma died three days after her husband.) The two are buried in the Garlow family plot northeast of the information plaza in the center of the cemetery—look for the large gray Garlow headstone. Included in the plot is the grave of her grandson (Buffalo Bill's great-grandson) Kit Cody, killed in a plane crash in Florida in 2013. *Address:* 1721 Gulch Avenue, Cody, Wyoming 82414. *Phone:* (307) 587-2411. *Website:* www.riversidecemeterydistrict.com.

About half a mile past the cemetery, you'll come to the South Fork Road (Highway 291). Follow this south for less than a mile to Robertson Street, and on the northeast corner you'll find a home once owned and occupied by Bill Cody. The home was built in 1902 for Buffalo Bill and was originally located behind the Irma Hotel. It was moved to its present location in 1972 and is today the **Buffalo**

The Buffalo Bill Cody's House Bed & Breakfast, formerly adjacent to the Irma Hotel where it was used by the Cody family.

Cedar Mountain and the Buffalo Bill Reservoir at Buffalo Bill State Park.

Bill Cody's House Bed & Breakfast. *Address:* 101 Robertson Street, Cody, Wyoming 82414. *Phone:* (307) 587-6169. *Website:* www.buffalobillcodybb.com.

Much farther down this road (and closed to the public) is **Cody's TE Ranch**. Cody used to hunt along the South Fork of the Shoshone, between the town and the ranch. After his death, the ranch was passed to Philadelphian Stanley Groves, who ranched but also used it as a family retreat, building cabins and an octagonal log library and game house at a distance from the original cabin. The property was later sold to Paul Patton of Kansas City, an associate of Tom Pendergast, who was forced to sell when Pendergast's political organization in Kansas City came under investigation. The next buyer was Robert W. Woodruff, then president and later board chairman of the Coca-Cola Company. In 1972 the property passed from Woodruff to another Coca-Cola executive, Charles Duncan, who continues to own the ranch today.

Always in view to the immediate south of U.S. 14/16 is **Cedar Mountain**, also known as Spirit Mountain, where Buffalo Bill wanted to be buried at the summit. The will he drew up in 1906 requested that location, to be marked with a massive red stone statue of a buffalo that would be visible from town. A later will, written in 1913, left all decisions to his wife, but he said again in a 1915 interview with the Omaha *World-Herald* that he planned to be buried here. He told the story of a smoke-like steam seen issuing from crevices on the mountain, what he joked "was from a fire being prepared for my last estate."

When he was buried in Colorado instead, the people of Cody were outraged and made several attempts to bring his body back. There's a story that several men from Cody succeeded in switching Buffalo Bill's body with that of another when it was in the Denver morgue and then brought it back to Wyoming for a secret burial on Cedar Mountain. But it's just a story: Mrs. Cody had Bill's coffin opened for viewing before his burial in Colorado.

Others are buried at the summit, however. An early Cody entrepreneur, Breck Moran, is buried here, flanked by a six-foot-tall fiberglass buffalo purportedly given by Golden, Colorado, as a peace offering for hosting Buffalo Bill's remains. The Indian-style grave marker of Buffalo Bill impersonator Ebb Tarr is nearby.

Locals discourage visiting the site, which is about four miles from the highway and involves hiking through private land. The author cannot verify the following directions to the summit (courtesy of www.summitpost.org): from the stoplight in front of Wal-Mart at the west end of Cody, travel west for 1.8 miles and turn left off of the highway onto Spirit Mountain Road. Stay left and begin heading up the mountain on the unpaved road. (This road is maintained, and the only time a four-wheel-drive vehicle would be absolutely necessary would be in the winter or in snowy conditions.) Continue on this road for 2.5 miles until the turnout on the right before the blue gate where the Spirit Mountain Cave sign is in view. This drive will take you from 5,100 feet at the base to 6,500 feet at the sign. (Cody would have visited this cave, which is today under lock and key. If you would like to explore it, visit the Bureau of Land Management at 1002 Blackburn Street for a permit or call 307-578-5900.)

To continue to Cody's planned gravesite, park here and walk the rest of the way. For the first two miles after the gate, the road crosses private property, so do not leave the road. There is another gate just before you reach the east summit and the large group of radio towers. When the road forks in the middle of the tower area, take the left turn and head west. After passing the last towers, the road veers left and drops one hundred feet before continuing up to the summit and the fiberglass buffalo.

A much easier site to access is back on U.S. 14/16, passing between Cedar and Rattlesnake Mountains. You're now coming up on the culmination of Bill Cody's efforts at irrigating the Bighorn Basin: the Shoshone Dam. In 1946, nearly thirty years after Cody's death and on the centennial of his birth, the dam and reservoir were renamed for Buffalo Bill. The **Buffalo Bill Dam and Visitor Center** is located six miles west of Cody on the route to Yellowstone National Park. You'll pass through several tunnels on the way—always a thrill when entering the mountains. Also impressive is the view from the top of the dam down the Shoshone River Canyon. Inside the visitor center are exhibits and a short film, including referral to Cody's work in irrigating the basin. *Hours:* Open daily, May through September. Weekdays, 8 A.M. to 6 P.M. (an hour later in the summer months); weekends, 9 A.M. to 5 P.M. *Admission:* Free. *Phone:* (307) 527-6076. *Website:* www.bbdvc.com.

The final stop of the "Cody Road" to Yellowstone lies about forty-five miles away. Cody's Wapiti Inn was torn down in 1913, but part of the materials

The Pahaska Tepee.

were used to expand the **Pahaska Tepee**, which still stands two miles from Yellowstone's east entrance in the heart of the Shoshone National Forest. Pahaska is described as a "complete mountain community" offering modern cabin-style rooms (including three cabins built during Cody's time), a full-service bar and restaurant, gift shop, fuel, convenience store, horseback riding (June through August), trout fishing, and cross-country skiing (December through March). The original "tepee" of the two-story log structure (listed on the National Register of Historic Places) is open for tours—be sure to check it out. Among the artifacts on display are historic flags, including a Cuban flag from San Juan Hill given by Theodore Roosevelt to Cody and a Monaco flag from that nation's prince after his visit. *Address:* 183 North Fork Highway, Cody, Wyoming 82414. *Phone:* (307) 527-7701. *Website:* www.pahaska.com.

Recommended Reading

William F. Cody's Wyoming Empire: The Buffalo Bill Nobody Knows by Robert E. Norman Bonner (OK: University of Oklahoma Press, 2007); *Buffalo Bill's Town in the Rockies: A Pictorial History of Cody, Wyoming* by Jeannie Cook (Virginia Beach, VA: Donning Company, 1996).

Denver and the End of the Trail

This is the last photograph of Buffalo Bill alive, in Glenwood Springs, Colorado, on January 3, 1917, one week before his passing.

After a visit to his family, friends, and properties in Wyoming, Buffalo Bill came to Denver in early December 1916 for a stay with his youngest sister, May, and her husband, Louis Decker, the manager of Buffalo Bill's Wild West.

Cody already had a long history with the city of Denver, from his gold-seeking as a young man through his scouting and showman days. He intended to use the time in the city to write autobiographical articles for the Hearst newspapers but caught a cold that was so severe that Lulu and Irma were summoned for fear of his death. He was up and walking before they got there.

On January 3, 1917, he went to Glenwood Springs, Colorado, to take in the town's mineral waters. While here, he posed for a photo—his last—on the porch of his friend, Dr. W. W. Crook. Cody suffered from a nervous collapse on January 5 and was brought back to May's home. Three days later came the public announcement that Buffalo Bill was dying.

Chauncey Thomas, a writer for *Outdoor Life* magazine and a friend of Cody, interviewed the old scout. "When the doctors told him that he would never see another sunset, Buffalo Bill dropped his head on his

May Cody Decker and her husband, Louis, at their home in 1893. This would become her brother Bill's final residence.

Thousands lined the sidewalk to the Colorado State Capitol to pay last respects to Buffalo Bill Cody.

breast for a moment, a long, still moment, then raised it, fearlessly and serene," wrote Thomas, as recounted by author Zane Grey. "Those eagle eyes, keen and kindly as ever they were, looked long at the mountains, snowy in the distance, then he quietly gave a few directions about his funeral, and then again became the knightly, genial man he had always been. The man was majestic."

Thomas said Cody spoke of his earlier life and of the military officers for whom he had scouted. They talked of his favorite gun—Lucretia Borgia—and of revolvers, knives, and buffalo hunting (Thomas was obviously asking questions for an outdoor magazine). They talked of Frank North and "Wild Bill" Hickok and the weapons they used, and then Cody's sister Julia said it was time for Thomas to go.

"The Old Scout was in pajamas and slippers, and over them had been a drawn house coat. Instantly Buffalo Bill was on his feet, straight as an Indian, head up, as in days of old . . . waxen pale, his silver hair flowing down over his straight, square shoulders, his hand out in the last farewell. . . . It was the last time. I knew it; he knew it; we all knew it. But on the surface not a sign."

On January 9, a Catholic priest visited Cody and baptized and received him into the church. This was probably strongly encouraged by his wife. Although he didn't belong to any organized church, Cody was said to be religious. He was raised a Methodist, attended Episcopal services, and donated to all of the churches built in his namesake town.

He began to sink rapidly on the morning of Wednesday, January 10, and fell into unconsciousness. Five minutes after noon, William F. "Buffalo Bill" Cody—the greatest plainsman the world had ever known—was dead.

The news of Cody's passing was felt with great sadness throughout the country but particularly on the Great Plains, where he had made his home and made so many friends. A public farewell was in order, and the Colorado State Capitol was the designated site. Cody's body was brought to the capitol on Monday morning, January 15, and a massive crowd was already queued outside the building to see him, including hundreds of boys and girls excused from school.

Bill's open casket rested at the foot of the staircase within the narrow rotunda and the mourners were politely, yet firmly urged along. The viewing hosted at least twenty-five thousand, with thousands more turned away. After a large procession through the streets of Denver, services followed at the local Elks Club. No burial would take place this day or in the immediate future—his casket was taken to Olinger's Mortuary to be placed in a crypt for burial on Decoration Day (today's Memorial Day).

There apparently was confusion over Cody's burial site. The Omaha *World-Herald* initially reported that he would probably be buried with his three children at Mount Hope Cemetery in Rochester, New York. Some speculated that Cody's family could not afford to return his body to Wyoming for burial and instead took the offer from the Masons and Elks to have him buried at Lookout Mountain west of Denver, near Golden.

Mourners pass before Cody's body in the capitol rotunda.

Lulu said Cody told her the day before he died that he wished to be buried on the mountain because it was pretty there and he could see four states. Some contend that Lulu was paid by Tammen and other interests to select the Colorado site because of the potential income it could generate.

The burial took place on June 3 rather than Decoration Day because the Grand Army of the Republic expressed concerns that its members would be unable to attend because of holiday parades. The Masons were primarily responsible for the funeral, driving the associated cars, guiding the traffic, and asking people not to cross the road carrying the procession. Newspapers reported that twenty to twenty-five thousand again paid their respects for Cody by making the seven-and-a-half-mile trek up Lookout Mountain on foot.

Louisa felt that with so many at the service to pay their respects they should be allowed to see Buffalo Bill one more time. She allowed the glass-topped casket to be opened and the mourners to pass and say good-bye to the great scout.

There were plans to raise funds for a grand mausoleum for Cody atop Lookout Mountain, spearheaded by the *Denver Post*. The effort was immediately politicized, and the proposed designs and the burial place were criticized. Since the United States had recently entered World War I, Louisa asked that the fundraising halt in order to focus on the national war effort. She died in 1921 and was buried alongside her husband. With inadequate funding and the passing of Mrs. Cody, efforts to build the monument withered.

That same year, Johnny Baker began the Buffalo Bill Memorial Museum and Pahaska Tepee next to the grave in order to display the hundreds of souvenirs he had gathered during his years with his foster father and the Wild West.

The Trail Today

May Cody lived at her two-story Queen Anne–style home until her death in 1926. The home changed hands a number of times until finally being converted into apartments. Poor remodeling jobs, neglect, and abandonment took their toll, and the house fell into such disrepair that it was slated for demolition in 1982.

That's when Denverite Gary Ice bought the home at 2932 Lafayette Street and went about the arduous task of restoring the **site of Buffalo Bill's death**. For about the next thirty years, he painstaking brought the stately Queen Anne house back to life, restoring its original configuration and many of the details appropriate to Cody's time period.

The house where Buffalo Bill died at 2932 Lafayette Street has been restored to its original glory.

Because of alterations in the house, it wasn't immediately known in which room Cody died, but Ice soon found out from newspaper accounts describing the second-floor room. It has since been decorated with photos, art, and newspaper accounts of Buffalo Bill. Friends sometimes spend the night there during visits. At press time, the home (a private residence with no public tours) was listed for sale.

Still standing in Denver along with May Cody's house, albeit a few stories taller, is the **Colorado State Capitol**. As you enter the building from the front entrance, past three steps identified as 5,280 feet above sea level (it was refigured a couple of times), you'll immediately see the grand staircase in the center of the first-floor rotunda. Cody's body lay in state at the foot of this staircase, and as you stand here, you're immediately struck with wonder at how twenty-five thousand people made it through the relatively confined space.

Current occupants of the home have decorated the room where Cody died with art and news clippings relating to his life and death in Denver.

Rotunda of the Colorado State Capitol.

Of course, there's more to see of the "mile-high" capitol than just the rotunda. The building is beautifully decorated throughout with Colorado rose onyx, a rare marble (the capitol consumed the entire supply). In fact, most of the structure is from Colorado-mined and quarried materials; only the ornamental brass, white oak woodwork, and marble stair treads and panels are from out of state. The dome is covered in 47.5 ounces of Colorado gold. Stained glass windows are located throughout the capitol on the second and third floors, and the dome contains the stained-glass portraits of sixteen inductees to the Colorado Hall of Fame who helped to establish the state.

The capitol offers a few different tours, including the historic, the legislative, and "Mr. Brown's Attic" (covering the early history and construction of the imposing building) tours—take in all three if you can. *Address:* 200 East Colfax Avenue, Denver, Colorado 80203. *Hours:* Monday through Friday, 7:30 A.M. to 5 P.M. *Phone:* (303) 866-2167 (tour desk). *Website:* www.colorado.gov/capitoltour.

After the viewing, Cody's body was taken to **Olinger's Mortuary** to be held until spring when he could be buried. Olinger's was in business until 1999 and hosted an estimated forty-five thousand funerals at its eighteen thousand-square-foot building with the giant blue neon sign. The mortuary is now gone, but beneath the sign is one of north Denver's trendy new restaurants, Linger. Drawing on the Olinger name and an invitation to take your time, today's Linger keeps the drinks chilled rather than the patrons. You can enjoy urban food staples and flavors from the Americas, Morocco, Turkey, Italy, Asia, and India, as well as beer and wine selections and interpretations of classic ethnic drinks. Weather permitting, take a table outdoors on the roof under the blue neon. *Address:* LoHiMarket Place Plaza, 2030 West 30th Avenue, Denver, Colorado 80211. *Phone:* (303) 993-3120. *Website:* lingerdenver.com.

Finally, Buffalo Bill Cody was taken to his final resting place on **Lookout Mountain**, overlooking the Great Plains and the Rocky Mountains, under the inscription reading "At rest here by his request" (for anyone from Wyoming, Nebraska, or elsewhere who thinks he should be buried in their state). The grave has become a very popular tourist site, as was expected,

Cody's grave on Lookout Mountain, where Louisa joined him in 1921.

with more than four hundred thousand annual visitors. Folks come here not only to visit the grave and take in the fantastic view, but also to visit the adjacent **Buffalo Bill Museum**, a fascinating repository of everything Buffalo Bill.

Now owned and operated by the city and county of Denver, the museum collects, cares for, and presents artifacts associated with Buffalo Bill and his life. There is plenty to see in historic photographs, paintings, and posters of Buffalo Bill and his presentations, as well as beautiful displays of firearms, clothing, souvenirs, a stuffed buffalo, a buffalo head, and much, much more. There are Winchesters that belonged to Cody, his favorite saddle, show outfits, and even Sitting Bull's headdress. It's easy to see why this was

Buckhorn Exchange.

named by *True West* magazine as its Museum of the Year in 2011.

Before you leave, the adjacent Pahaska Tepee café and gift shop has about anything you'd want in Buffalo Bill souvenirs and books—and it's where to go for a real buffalo burger. *Address:* 987½ Lookout Mountain Road, Golden, Colorado 80401. *Hours:* May 1 to October 31—museum open daily, 9 A.M. to 5 P.M.; café and gift shop open daily, 8:30 A.M. to sunset. November 1 to April 30—museum open Tuesday to Sunday, 9 A.M. to 4 P.M.; café and gift shop open, 9 A.M. to sunset. *Admission:* Adults $5, seniors $4, children 6 to 15 $1, children 5 and under free. *Phone:* (303) 526-0744. *Website:* www.buffalobill.org.

Related Sites

Buffalo Bill presented at least thirty-five times in Denver and elsewhere in Colorado. He had many friends here and—at least during his drinking days—visited many a saloon. One of those friends was Henry Zietz, who met Cody in 1875 when he was but a ten-year-old and who later joined Cody as a scout. As part of Buffalo Bill's Wild West, Sitting Bull called him "Shorty Scout" because of his height. In 1893 Zietz opened the **Buckhorn Exchange**, a saloon which catered to cattlemen, miners, railroaders, silver barons, Indian chiefs, gamblers, businessmen, and old friends like William F. Cody. It got its name from Zietz's business of exchanging railroaders' paychecks for gold, along with a token good for a free lunch and beer—and how many railroaders stopped at one beer? Answer: not many.

The Buckhorn Exchange today is Denver's oldest restaurant. There are hundreds of mounted big game heads, firearms, historic photos, and other memorabilia throughout the restaurant. Ask for seating in the Buffalo Bill Room to be surrounded with items related to the great scout as well as buffalo heads. Upstairs is the Buckhorn's ornate white-oak bar, built in Germany in 1857 and brought to America by the Zietz family; Buffalo Bill would have bent an elbow at this bar. This is a fun and fascinating Cody gem in Denver, and the food is great, too. Reservations recommended. *Address:* 1000 Osage Street, Denver, Colorado 80204. *Phone:* (303) 534-9505. *Website:* www.buckhorn.com.

Remembering
Buffalo Bill

William "Buffalo Bill" Cody in 1910.

As described in the previous chapter, the initial efforts to memorialize Cody gained little traction. The proposed designs for his mausoleum and the location of his burial place attracted criticism. Louisa asked that fundraising stop while the United States focused on World War I. Death then took many of those closest to Cody. Maj. John Burke lived only thirteen weeks after Bill, dying in April 1917. Bill's daughter, Irma, and her husband, Fred Garlow, died in October 1918. And Louisa died in October 1921.

The Buffalo Bill Memorial Museum and Pahaska Tepee set up by Johnny Baker next to Cody's grave did take off, with a display of souvenirs and other items. As this attraction proved to be incredibly popular, it could be said to have created a whole new generation of Cody family dysfunction.

Buffalo Bill's niece Mary Jester Allen and other relatives established the Cody Family Association in Chicago and announced plans to bring Buffalo Bill's body to Cody. His sisters Julia and May immediately spoke out against the proposal, and Baker said the move was made by "people who had nothing else to talk about." Allen wrote letters to family and friends criticizing Baker and his museum. In response, Baker reburied the Codys under twelve feet of reinforced concrete.

Allen had already commissioned "The Scout" statue for installation in Cody, and in 1926 the family association announced plans to establish not one but two museums dedicated to Buffalo Bill's memory. Denver and Cheyenne were once identified as potential sites, but the board ultimately decided on Cody and Omaha. Cody would include relics and paraphernalia of his scouting days in Wyoming while Omaha would cover his pioneer life and buffalo-hunting feats on the Plains. Plans for the Omaha museum ultimately fell apart, and the entire collection went to Cody. That museum, replicating the ranch house at the TE Ranch, opened in 1927 and eventually grew into today's Buffalo Bill Center of the West.

In 1946, one hundred years after William F. Cody's birth, the Shoshone Dam and Reservoir was renamed as Buffalo Bill Dam and Reservoir by act of Congress and the signature of President Harry Truman.

The centennial of Cody's birth gave no indication the dispute was over, however. His grandson William Garlow, representing Wyoming, said, "If grandfather were alive he would say, 'Get my remains out from under this concrete even if you have to quarry me out.'" Denver's Fred Steinhauer, who came up with the idea of adding fifteen tons of concrete and iron over Cody's grave, responded, "They couldn't get the old boy out with an atomic bomb. No man was ever buried better. He won't even hear Gabriel's horn."

William F. Cody in the Nebraska Hall of Fame.

Although it didn't receive an "official" museum, Nebraska remembered its favorite son. Scout's Rest Ranch became a state park and historic house museum in North Platte in 1965. Four years later, William F. "Buffalo Bill" Cody was inducted as a member of the Nebraska Hall of Fame, with his bust installed in the Nebraska State Capitol in Lincoln.

And then there are the festivals. All of his Great Plains hometowns (except for his birthplace) hold a celebration in honor of Buffalo Bill, and there's even one where a connection doesn't seem possible.

Leavenworth, Kansas, has its Buffalo Bill Days Festival (www.buffalobill festival.com) in mid-September. Nebraskaland Days and the Buffalo Bill

Rodeo (www.nebraskalanddays.com) take place in June across the road from the Scout's Rest Ranch in North Platte. Cody, Wyoming, holds the Buffalo Bill Art Show & Sale (www.buffalobillartshow.com) annually. Down the mountainside from Lookout Mountain, Golden, Colorado, has its Buffalo Bill Days (www.buffalobilldays.com) in late July.

Finally, every August, Lanesboro in southeast Minnesota celebrates its own Buffalo Bill Days (www.lanesboro-mn.gov). According to the organizers, Cody began the Wild West show there in 1900 with himself and ten other performers. That contradicts known history about Buffalo Bill: the record doesn't even have him making a tour stop in Lanesboro, let alone starting the Wild West there. But given the fun and success Buffalo Bill had with his legends, who's to begrudge a town from doing the same?

APPENDIX
Quotations of William F. Cody

The following quotations from William F. Cody, compiled by Dr. John Rumm, curator of the Buffalo Bill Museum at the Buffalo Bill Center of the West, offer insight into the man who presented himself as "Buffalo Bill." Some of these he would have said as "Bill," and others as Cody—the plainsman, businessman, entertainer, and American—but all of them reflect how he lived and what he believed.

on Advertising

At one time, about twelve or fifteen years ago, I got the notion that I was so well-known that the money I spent on advertising was a clean waste of the good old long green. So I checked up for a while, but not for long. I found my personality wasn't half such an advertising card as I thought it was. And so I got back into the advertising game stronger than ever, and I've never regretted it. No man who has any keen realization of the necessities of modern times will ever overlook the advantage of advertising.

"Famous Scout, 'Pioneer Publicity Man,'
Is Applauded as He Recounts Western Tales and
Boosts Indian Council," n.d., BB Scrapbooks

on Ambition

I am never going down. I am always going up.

Young Will Cody, as recalled by
Julia Cody Goodman in her memoirs

There is a barrel of money in sight, and I am after the barrel.

Interview, *North Platte Tribune*,
January 3, 1894

on America

I am American enough to think that we can do almost anything if we once make up our minds that it has to be done.

Interview, April 1899

on American Indians

General Sheridan gave me credit for doing a great deal of work in 1876, but I felt I was doing wrong to fight the Indians. I've lived in the Indian country for thirty years and I've never known a treaty to be kept by the whites yet. The Indians have been driven from the Atlantic to the Pacific. They are badly treated.

Quoted in the Philadelphia
Sunday Times, July 5, 1885

They have as good a natural right to vote as anybody. They have been Americans for some time, and I know they would appreciate the confidence placed in them. Besides, it is the only way I know to get into Congress.

Interview, August 1888

on the American West

The West was, in the early 1850s, the young man's opportunity. It is the young man's opportunity to-day more than ever.

Interview, May 1908

The West is settled by people who do things, and that is one of the reasons I like it. . . . A Westerner in the East soon gets tired of the confinement. He wants to get out and do things.

Quoted in "Cody with Poor Richards,"
Philadelphia Inquirer, April 6, 1911

What chance has a person to broaden in a city, with its narrow streets and brick walls? You have to go West to find room in which to do that. Why, out here, you throw out your arms and holler! You feel so good, you just have to holler. You're glad you're alive, and you're thanking God you're in a healthful country.

Interview in "Gone is the Wild West,"
Fort Worth Telegram, April 15, 1911

There's no more wild West. The last of it went when I settled up the Big Horn basin.

Interview in "Gone is the Wild West,"
Fort Worth Telegram, April 15, 1911

on "Buffalo Bill"

[Upon being accosted by a cavalry officer who said Buffalo Bill shouldn't scalp Indians]

Gentlemen, I want you to understand one thing: the Honorable William F. Cody does not scalp Indians. But when I am on the plains I am Buffalo Bill, and Buffalo Bill scalps them every time.

"The Hon. Mr. Cody and 'Buffalo Bill,'"
Rocky Mountain News, July 9, 1889

on Buffalo Bill's Wild West

I have more callers among men who think I ought to remember them because they were on the plains at the same time. They will ask me to remember meeting them at the same time the Pacific railroad was completed. Enquiry as to where they saw me will probably result in the fact that they were in an emigrant wagon and when I ask where they saw me, they will probably say in a palace car.

Interview, June 1896

I wanted to take my show to all the little towns in Nebraska, Colorado and Kansas before I quit the show business. I didn't expect to make a cent of money on the trip. I went because I was always getting letters from old-timers asking me why I didn't ever visit them with my show. But I made money hand over fist. People drove 300 miles to see my show. They came so fast that their cows went dry before they got back home. Yes, that's a fact. I got letters from 'em telling me their cows went dry.

Interview, October 1898

on Character

An old gentleman kept staring at me while I was engaged with my correspondence in a New York hotel. When finished, I just went up to him, and I said, "Well, friend, and what do you think of it." "Oh, he says," "I thought I would see a man about 20 feet high, and with horns."

"A Chat with Colonel Cody,"
Bruce Herald, March 4, 1892

on Fame and Fortune

I have captured the country from the Queen down—am doing them to the tune of $10,000 a day. Talk about show business! There never was anything like it ever known, and never will be again, and with my European reputation you can easily guess the business I will do when I get back to my own country. It's pretty hard work with two and three performances a day and the society racket at receptions, dinners, &c. No man—not even Grant—was received better than your humble servant. I have dined with every one of the royalty, from Albert, Prince of Wales, down. I sometimes wonder if it is the same old Bill Cody, the bullwhacker. Well, Colonel, I still wear the same sized hat, and when I make my pile I am coming back to visit all the old boys. If you meet any of them tell them I ain't got the big head worth a cent. I am over here for dust.

To William Ray, June 23, 1887

A fortune is what we are after, and we'll at least give this wheel a turn or two and see what luck we have.

The Life of Hon. William F. Cody (published 1879)

on Long Hair

I do hate long hair, but people have come to identify me with long hair so I won't cut it. Long hair is business and an art with me.

Interview, April 1898

on Military

There are no men in the world who can do so much on so little as the American troops. They can subsist on nothing and go on fighting. After our men become thoroughly acclimated, a handful will be more than a match for an army of barbarians.

Interview, April 1899

on Progress

Do not think that I am one of those who deplore the days that are gone. Far be it from me to do that. It is the necessary change teeming with big results. The play must go on from scene to scene.

Interview, May 1908

Times certainly have changed, but they have changed for better things.

Quoted in "Buffalo Bill Now Drives an Auto,"
Nashville Tennessean and the Nashville American, May 30, 1915

on Retirement

I was born on the frontier, and all my early life I lived on it. When the towns followed us, we moved further on, and so kept clear of them. That's what I want to get back to. I want to ride my horse on the plains, not in the arena. I want to look my mother Nature in the face again, and shake hands with her in her home.

Interview, *St. James Gazette*
(England), September 28, 1892

Back to the New West. The Wild West I leave with you.

Handwritten across "How Buffalo Bill
Is to Spend His Time," ca. 1910

on Riding and the Rough Riders

A man to ride at all comfortably must sit up straight, expanding his lungs to their fullest capacity, thus getting the full benefit of the ozone, and making it the healthiest of all exercises. In a word, while I am not opposed to bicycling, I believe horseback-riding to be far superior as a recreation and as an exercise.

Interview, May 1896

You know, I originated the name "Rough Riders." I have been calling my men Rough Riders for ten years. Why should I continue to call them rough? Next year I am going to call them "Smooth Riders." They're the smoothest riders on earth.

Interview, Kansas City, October 1898

on Show Business
and his Theatrical Career

[In the early 1870s] I was a government scout. I could make nothing more than a meager living at that and I yearned for something to do whereby I might be enabled to educate my children properly. I determined to star on the road with a dramatic company. I had but $3 in my pocket, but I got forty people together, and started making money from the first night's stand. I was soon in good shape. After I had become reasonably well fixed, I might have given up the business, but it was so big I couldn't let go.

Interview, May 1896

I didn't try to act. I did what I used to do on the prairie, not what I thought some other fellow might have done if he felt that way.

Interview, September 1892

The plays and the acting were so bad that they were actually good. I appeared in a number of border dramas, and that I did not lose my life has always been a marvel to me—not from the use of real bullets instead of blank cartridges, but from some member of an irate audience.

Interview, May 1908

on War and Peace

War is a terrible thing. . . . I have been personally presented to and have become personally acquainted with every crowned head of the fighting nations. I have seen all those peoples in the quiet pursuits of peace. I know what war means over there [in Europe]. It is not a war of individuals this time, but a war of the most destructive agencies and elements ever handled by mankind. In my opinion it is not possible for such a war to last long, for they will be exhausted. So destructive is it that no sane person will ever think of starting another war. That will mean universal, everlasting peace.

Remarks on Prohibition and universal peace rally,
Oklahoma City, October 1914, quoted in
"Grapho," "Temperance Tide in the Southwest,"
The Congregationalist and Christian World, Oct. 22, 1914

William F. Cody's Rules to Live By
[aka "The Cody Code"]

Aphorisms taken from Cody's letters, speeches, and interviews.

- *Wait until you get there, and then fire right out in the usual way.*
- *Don't ford the river until you get to it.*
- *Be a stayer—never give up!*
- *I never feel blue. When I have any losses, I just make up my mind to let the past be gone and forget the past and build up the future.*
- *I am different from a man who spends his life always in one town. My business and my life compel me to move often and quickly.*
- *A man never gets to the top if the opportunity does not present itself.*
- *I always look to the comfort and the support of my family first and above all things.*
- *Any day may change your luck.*
- *Contentment and hope—without hope one is dead.*
- *Do good, and make others happy.*
- *A man don't want to get used to being too luxurious, because it makes him lazy and good for nothing.*
- *What's the use of talking? I won't have long-winded debates. Get down to action—that's what is needed.*
- *I believe in shooting at the first sight. If you don't, you're going to miss. I'll hit 48 out of 50 shots because I pulled the trigger at first sight.*
- *I don't like being kept up late. No, sir, I'd rather get to bed early at night. I have to do 18 hours' work a day, and I can't afford to loaf.*

Bibliography

Books

Barnes, Jeff. *Forts of the Northern Plains.* Mechanicsburg, PA: Stackpole Books, 2008.
———. *The Great Plains Guide to Custer.* Mechanicsburg, PA: Stackpole Books, 2012.
Brill, Charles J. *Custer, Black Kettle, and the Fight on the Washita.* Norman: University of Oklahoma Press, 1938.
Carmichael, Dr. John B. and Bob Rea. *Fort Supply: The Hub of the Military Roads and Trails of the Southern Great Plains.* Fort Supply: Historic Fort Supply Foundation, 2001.
Carriker, Robert. *Fort Supply: Indian Territory.* Norman: University of Oklahoma Press, 1970.
Cody, William F. *The Life of Hon. William F. Cody, Known as Buffalo Bill.* Lincoln: University of Nebraska Press, 1978.
Custer, Elizabeth B. *Boots and Saddles: or, Life in Dakota with General Custer.* Norman: University of Oklahoma Press, new edition 1961.
———. *Tenting on the Plains: General Custer in Kansas and Texas.* New York: Barnes & Noble Publishing, 2006.
Custer, Gen. George A. *My Life on the Plains.* Lincoln: University of Nebraska Press, 1966.
DeLano, Patti. *Kansas, Off the Beaten Path.* Guilford, CT: The Globe Pequot Press, 2001.
Ellenbrook, Edward Charles. *Outdoor and Trail Guide to the Wichita Mountains of Southwest Oklahoma.* Lawton, OK: In-the-Valley-of-the-Wichita House, 1983.
Faulk, Odie B. *Dodge City, the Most Western Town of All.* New York: Oxford University Press, 1977.
Federal Writers Project. *The WPA Guide to 1930s Kansas.* Lawrence: University Press of Kansas, 1984.
Greene, Jerome A. *Fort Randall on the Missouri, 1856–1892.* Pierre: South Dakota Historical Society Press, 2005.
———. *Indian War Veterans: Memories of Army Life and Campaigns in the West, 1864–1898.* El Dorado Hills, CA: Savas Beatie, 2007.
———. *Yellowstone Command: Colonel Nelson A. Miles and the Great Sioux War 1876–1877.* Lincoln: University of Nebraska Press, 1991.
Griffith, T.D. *South Dakota.* New York: Compass American Guides, 2004.
Hart, Herbert M. *Old Forts of the Northwest.* New York: Bonanza Books, 1963.
———. *Old Forts of the Southwest.* —, 1964.

———. *Tour Guide to Old Western Forts.* Boulder: Pruett Publishing Company, 1980.

Hedren, Paul L. *First Scalp for Custer: The Skirmish at Warbonnet Creek, Nebraska, July 17, 1876.* Lincoln: University of Nebraska Press, 1980.

———. *Great Sioux War Orders of Battle: How the United States Army Waged War on the Northern Plains, 1876–1877.* Norman: Arthur H. Clark Company, 2011.

———. *Ho! For the Black Hills: Captain Jack Reports the Black Hills Gold Rush and Great Sioux War.* Pierre: South Dakota Historical Society Press, 2012.

———. *Traveler's Guide to the Great Sioux War.* Helena, Montana: Historical Society Press, 1996.

Holmes, Louis A. *Fort McPherson, Nebraska. Fort Cottonwood, N.T. Guardian of the Tracks and Trails.* Lincoln: Johnsen Publishing Company, 1963.

Hughes, J. Patrick. *Fort Leavenworth: Gateway to the West.* Topeka: Kansas State Historical Society, 2000.

Hutton, Paul Andrew, ed. *The Custer Reader.* Lincoln: University of Nebraska Press, 1992.

Jennewein, J. Leonard and Jane Boorman, editors. *Dakota Panorama.* Sioux Falls, SD: Brevet Press, 1973.

Kinsey, Maxine Schuurmans. *The Sioux City to Fort Randall Military Road 1856–1892, Revisited.* Sioux Falls, SD: Pine Hill Press, 2010.

Mackintosh, Donald P., publisher. *Brevet's South Dakota Historical Markers.* Sioux Falls: Brevet Press, 1974.

———. *Brevet's North Dakota Historical Markers.* —, 1975.

McKale, William and Robert Smith. *Images of America: Fort Riley (Kansas).* Charleston: Arcadia Publishing, 2009.

McKale, William and William D. Young. *Fort Riley: Citadel of the Frontier West.* Topeka: Kansas State Historical Society, 2000.

Michno, Gregory F. *Encyclopedia of Indian Wars, Western Battles and Skirmishes, 1850–1890.* Missoula, MT: Mountain Press Publishing Company, 2003.

Michno, Gregory F. and Susan J. *Forgotten Fights: Little-Known Raids and Skirmishes on the Frontier, 1823 to 1890.* Missoula, MT: Mountain Press Publishing Company, 2008.

Moeller, Bill and Jan. *The Pony Express: A Photographic History.* Missoula, MT: Mountain Press Publishing Company, 2002.

Morgan, R. Kent. *Our Hallowed Ground: Guide to Indian War Battlefield Locations in Eastern Montana.* Bloomington, IN: Author House, 2004.

Nye, Col. W.S. *Carbine and Lance: The Story of Old Fort Sill.* Norman: University of Oklahoma Press, 1937.

Oliva, Leo E. *Fort Dodge: Sentry of the Western Plains.* Topeka: Kansas State Historical Society, 1998.

———. *Fort Harker: Defending the Journey West.* —, 2000.

———. *Fort Hays, Frontier Army Post.* —, 1980.

———. *Fort Hays: Keeping Peace on the Plains.* —, 1996.

———. *Fort Larned: Guardian of the Santa Fe Trail.* —, 1997.

———. *Fort Wallace: Sentinel on the Smoky Hill Trail.* —, 1998.

Prucha, Francis Paul. *Atlas of American Indian Affairs.* Lincoln: University of Nebraska Press, 1990.

Schuler, Harold H. *Fort Sully: Guns at Sunset.* Vermillion: University of South Dakota Press, 1992.

Settle, Raymond W. and Mary Lund. *Saddles and Spurs: The Pony Express Saga.* Lincoln: University of Nebraska Press, 1972.

Sherman, Lt. Gen. P.H. *Outline Descriptions of the Posts in the Military Division of the Missouri.* Bellevue, NE: The Old Army Press, facsimile edition 1969.

Stewart, Edgar I. *Custer's Luck.* Norman: University of Oklahoma Press, 1955.

Utley, Robert M. *Cavalier in Buckskin: George Armstrong Custer and the Western Military Frontier.* Norman: University of Nebraska Press, 1988.

Utley, Robert M., editor. *Encyclopedia of the American West.* New York: Wings Books, 1997.

Waldman, Carl. *Atlas of the North American Indian.* New York: Facts on File, 1985.

Walton, George. *Sentinel of the Plains: Fort Leavenworth and the American West.* Englewood Cliffs, NJ: Prentice-Hall, 1973.

Wilson, Steve. *Oklahoma Treasures and Treasure Tales.* Norman: University of Oklahoma Press, 1976.

Wishart, David J., editor. *Encyclopedia of the Great Plains.* Lincoln: University of Nebraska Press, 2004.

Wright, Muriel H., et al. *His Imperial Highness The Grand Duke Alexis in the United States of America During the Winter of 1871–72.* Cambridge: Riverside Press, 1872.

———. *Mark of Heritage: Oklahoma's Historic Sites.* Norman: University of Oklahoma Press, 1976.

Newspapers

Daily State Journal (Lincoln, NE)
> January 17, 1872. "North Platte, Neb., January 15. The Grand Duke's buffalo hunt has proved a grand success . . ."
> January 19, 1872. "North Platte, January 16. Yesterday the second and last day of the imperial buffalo hunt . . ."

New York Herald
> January 16, 1872. "The Imperial Buffalo Hunter. General Sheridan and the Grand Duke on the Prairies."

Omaha Herald
> January 14, 1872. "The Grand Duke, Alexis, was duly welcomed at Omaha . . ."
> January 16, 1872. "North Platte, January 13. The Grand Duke and party arrived . . ."

Government Publications

Utley, Robert M. *Little Bighorn Battlefield: A History and Guide to the Battle of the Little Bighorn.* Washington, D.C.: National Park Service, 1988.

Utley, Robert M., et al. *Soldier and Brave: Historic Places Associated with Indian Affairs and the Indian Wars in the Trans-Mississippi West.* Washington, D.C.: National Park Service, 1971.

Atlases

Kansas Atlas & Gazetteer. Yarmouth, ME: DeLorme, 2003.
Montana Atlas & Gazetteer. ———, 2001.
Nebraska Atlas & Gazetteer. ———, 2005.
North Dakota Atlas & Gazetteer. ———, 1999.
Oklahoma Atlas & Gazetteer. ———, 2003.
South Dakota Atlas & Gazetteer. ———, 2004.
Texas Atlas & Gazetteer. ———, 1995.
Wyoming Atlas & Gazetteer. ———, 2001.

Miscellaneous Publications, Guides, Brochures, Pamphlets, and Maps

Barton County (Kansas) Historical Society Museum and Village.
Blackburn, Col. Forrest R. *Cantonment Leavenworth, 1827 to 1832.* Fort Leavenworth Historical Society (Reprint from *Military Review*, Dec. 1971).
Custer National Cemetery. Tucson, AZ: Southwest Parks & Monuments Association, 1994.
Custer Trail Auto Tour. USDA Forest Service.
Dodge City–Santa Fe Trail–Fort Dodge Self-Guided Tour. Dodge City Convention & Visitors Bureau.
Ellsworth County Historical Society.
Fort Harker Museum Complex. Ellsworth County Historical Society.
Fort Hays State Historic Site. Kansas Historical Society.
Fort Larned Official Map and Guide. Washington, D.C.: Government Printing Office: 1984.
Fort Riley 2007 Guide and Telephone Directory. Anchorage, AK: AQP Publishing, 2007.
Fort Riley 2008 Installation Map. Anchorage, AK: AQP Publishing, 2008.
Fort Riley's Historic Buildings. The U.S. Cavalry Museum.
Fort Supply Historic Site. Oklahoma Historical Society.
Fort Wallace Memorial Museum. Fort Wallace Memorial Association.
Historic Custer House, Quarters 24, Fort Riley, KS. U.S. Cavalry Museum and the Fort Riley Historical and Archaeological Society.
Historic Fort Dodge: Sentinel on the Santa Fe Trail. Kansas Soldiers' Home
Historic Main Post Walking Tour, Fort Riley, Kansas. Museum Division, Fort Riley, Kansas.
Historic Mobeetie. Texas Historical Commission.
Lawton/Fort Sill Oklahoma Visitors and Resource Guide. Lawton/Fort Sill Chamber of Commerce.
Little Bighorn Battlefield National Monument Official Map and Guide. Washington, D.C.: Government Printing Office: 1994.
Little Bighorn National Monument. Tuscon, AZ: Western National Parks Association, 1996.
Paine, Judge Bayard H. "The Famous Buffalo Hunt of Grand Duke Alexis of Russia."
Prairie County Horizons. Undaunted Stewardship.
Quartz Mountain Park History. Quartz Mountain Resort.
Reno–Benteen Entrenchment Trail. Tuscon, AZ: Western National Parks Association, 2002.
Santa Fe Trail Center Historical Museum & Library.
Santa Fe Trail Official Map and Guide. Washington, D.C.: Government Printing Office: 2004.

Self-Guided Tour of Fort Leavenworth, the Gateway to the West. Fort Leavenworth Historical Society.

Shoemaker, Col. John O. *The Custer Court-Martial.* Fort Leavenworth Historical Society (Reprint from *Military Review,* Oct. 1971).

Southwest Oklahoma's Great Plains Country, 2010 Travel Guide. Great Plains Country Association.

Up Pawnee Fork. Fort Larned Old Guard.

Washita Battlefield National Historic Site Trail Guide. Western National Parks Association.

Washita Battlefield Official Map and Guide. Washington, D.C.: Government Printing Office: 2009.

Websites

Kyvig, David E. "The Handbook of Texas Online: Fort Elliott." Texas State Historical Association. www.tshaonline.org.

Unpublished Sources

McNally, Jim. "A Romanoff Roams the Rockies in 1872." University of Colorado at Denver, 1984.

Index

Page numbers in italics indicate illustrations and sidebars.

Adair, Samuel and Florella, 13
Adams Museum, *19*
Albright, Horace, 183
Alderdice, Susanna, 71
Alexander Majors Historic House
　and Museum, 24–25
Alexandrovich, Alexei, Grand Duke
　of Russia, 88–92, *89, 109*
Allen, Mary Jester, 202
American Pickers (TV program), 5
Anthony, Susan B., gravesite, 99
Antique Archaeology, 5
Armes, George A., 44–45, *45*
Arthur, Chester A., 159
Ash Hollow State Historical
　Park, 26
Augur, Christopher C., 75

Bailey, James, 161
　death of, 163
Baker, Johnny, 159, *163*, 196, 202
Baker, Olive, *105*
"Battle of the Bills" hunting contest,
　59–60
　site of, *62*
Battle of Lexington State Historic
　Site, 42
Beck, George T., 179
Bennett, James Gordon, *80*, 80–81
Big Horn Expedition, 65–68

Black Hills Rangers, *118*
Brackenridge, William F., 2
Bratt, John, 128
Brown, John, 13
Bucher's Saloon, *147, 149*
Buckhorn Exchange, 200, *200*
"Buffalo Bill"
　the first, *58*
　others with nickname, 57–59
Buffalo Bill, the King of Border Men
　(magazine serial and play), 95
Buffalo Bill Center of the West,
　184–87, 202
　restored stagecoach at, *186*
Buffalo Bill Cody Park, 10
Buffalo Bill Cody's House Bed &
　Breakfast, *188*, 188–89
Buffalo Bill Combination, 97–98,
　128–29
Buffalo Bill Cultural Center, 62
Buffalo Bill Dam and Reservoir,
　202
Buffalo Bill Dam and Visitor
　Center, 190
Buffalo Bill Memorial Museum and
　Pahaska Tepee, 196, 202
Buffalo Bill Museum, 4–5, 165,
　199–200
Buffalo Bill Ranch State Historical
　Park, 141–42

Buffalo Bill State Park, Cedar
   Mountain and Buffalo Bill
   Reservoir at, *189*
Buffalo Bill's Cave, 25, *25*
Buffalo Bill's Wild West, 135, 158–65
   birthplace of, 147
   Cavalry Maze, *159*
   Indians of, *158*
   overseas trip, 160–61
   recommended reading, 165
   running, *162–63*
   sites, 165
   see also Wild West
"Buffalo Bill—The Scout" statue,
   187, *187*
buffalo hunting and hunts, 55–60,
   56, 62, 79–83
   Miles 1892, 81–83
   millionaires, 80–81
   royal, 88–93, *89, 92*
   sites, 83–84
Buntline, Ned, 95, *95, 96*
Burke, John M., 97, *162*
   and Cody at Pine Ridge
      Reservation, *174*
   death of, 202

Camp Alexis, commemorative
   marker, *92*
Camp Robinson, *102*
Canary, Martha "Calamity Jane," *19*
Carr, Eugene A., 47–49, 64, *72,* 101
   Battle of Summit Springs and, 71–76
Carson, Kit, 39
Carver, W. F. "Doc," 145, *145*
Cedar Mountain, planned gravesite at,
   189, 189–90
Chimney Rock State Historic Site,
   33, *34*
Christ Episcopal Church, 129–30, *130*
Civil War
   Cody's activities during, 39–42
   recommended reading, 42
   sites, 42

Clark, Ben, 82, *82*
Cliff, Charles, as guest for dedication
   of Pony Express monument, *30*
Cody, Arta, *182*
   birth of, 44
   death of, 163, 180
   with parents, *132*
Cody, Eliza, 8
Cody, Irma, *182*
   birth of, 135
   death of, 202
Cody, Isaac, 2–4
   attack on, 9, *9*
   burial of, *11*
   Connelley on, 10
   death of, 10
Cody, Julia, 2
Cody, Kit Carson, 98, *98*
   death of, 98
Cody, Laura Ella, 8
Cody, Louisa Frederici, *40,* 41, *41*
   with Bill, *181*
   with Bill and Arta, *132*
   Bill relationship, 128, 137, 180–81
   with daughters, *182*
   death of, 196, 202
Cody, Martha O'Connor, 2
Cody, Mary Ann Laycock, 2, *11*
   burial of, *11*
   death of, 39
Cody, May, 8
Cody, Orra, death of, 135
Cody, Rebecca Sumner, 2
Cody, Samuel, 2
   death of, 4
   gravesite, 6, *6*
Cody, William Frederick "Buffalo Bill,"
   18, 63, 96, 115
   at age eleven, *14*
   at age four, *1*
   bad investments made by, 164
   in Bighorn Basin, Wyoming, 179–83
   birthplace of, 6
   boyhood home, *4,* 5–6

buffalo hunting, 45, 55–60, *56*, *62*
burial site, 195–96
and Burke at Pine Ridge
    Reservation, *174*
cabinet card for, *157*
as cattle rancher, 127–28
childhood, 2–4
confusion and mystery concerning
    life of, xiii
Crawford relationship, *118–19*
creating historical films, 174
Custer relationship, *108–9*
death of, 195
as dispatch rider and guide for
    Sherman, 41
in 1870s, *126*
in 1880s, *144*
in 1890s, *178*
encountering Indians near Prairie
    Dog Creek, *20*
in entertainment business, 127
favorite stories concerning, xiii
first dime novel written by, 98
"first scalp for Custer" depiction, *104*
at Fort McPherson, 64–68, *78*
founding a town, 45
with friends and fellow
    performers, *150*
funeral, *194*, 195, *195*
gravesite, 198–99, *199*
as guest for dedication of Pony
    Express monument, *30*
as guide and courier for Hazen, 46
as guide on royal buffalo hunt,
    88–92
as guide and scout for Ninth Kansas
    Volunteers, 39
homestead, 5, 6, 10
house died at, 196–97, *197*
as hunting guide, 79–83
with Indians of the Wild West, *158*
jewelry made for, 92
joined Red Legged Scouts, 39
as justice of the peace, *65*

last appearance in Buffalo Bill's
    Wild West, 165
last buffalo killed by, *82–83*
last days as scout, 116–21
last photograph of, *192*
with Louisa, *40*, 181
with Louisa and Arta, *132*
Louisa relationship, 128, 137, 180–81
marriage of, 41
Medals of Honor, *66–67*
and Miles viewing Indian camp, *172*
mustered into service, 40
nickname, 57–59
in 1910, *201*
in North Platte, Nebraska, 134–38
in outfit worn at Warbonnet, *100*
overcoat given to, 92
photographed by Edric Eaton, *91*
Pony Express career, 28–30
as private in Seventh Kansas
    Volunteer Cavalry, *38*
promotional poster, *88*
quotations of, 205–11
rank titles, *175*
with rifle "Lucretia Borgia," *55*
scalping of Yellow Hair
    reenactment, *104*
as scout, *43*, 44–49
in scouting garb, *94*
with Sitting Bull cabinet card, *166*
on the stage, 95–99
starting town named Rome, 56–57
and Tall Bull death, 72–76
at time of royal buffalo hunt, *87*
in uniform as colonel, *175*
at Wounded Knee, 173–74
wounding of, 48
Yellow Hair death, 104–7
as youth, 15–20
Cody, Wyoming, 179–83
    recommended reading, 191
    sites, 183–91, *185*
Cody Canal, 183–85
Cody City, Wyoming, 179, 183

Cody Enterprise, 179, 183
Cody Family Association, 202
Cody House, 98
Cody and North Ranch, 127–28, 130–31
 house, *131*
 postcard, *128*
 sites, 129–30
Cody Park, 141
Cody Road to Yellowstone, 183–91
Collins, Caspar, 35–36
Colorado mining expedition, 20, 21
Colorado State Capitol, 197–98
 rotunda of, *198*
Columbus, Nebraska, 145–47
 sites, 147–49
Comstock, William "Medicine Bill," *59*, 59–60
Connelley, William E., 19
 on Isaac Cody, 10
Conquering the Wilderness (Triplett), 45
Constitution Hall State Historic Site, 13
Crawford, John "Captain Jack," 116, *119*
 Cody relationship, *118–19*
Crook, George, *116*
Crook, W. W., 193
Custer, George Armstrong, 24, 54, 88, *89*, 90
 Cody meeting, 44
 Cody relationship, *108–9*
 with Grand Duke Alexis, *109*

Davies, Henry Eugene, 80–81
Deadwood, South Dakota, *19*
Decker, May Cody and Louis, 193, *193*
Devil's Gate Station, 36
"dime novels," 95
Douglass, Frederick, gravesite, 99

Eaton, Edric, 151
1876 Sioux Campaign, 101–7, 116–21
 recommended reading, 114
 sites, *106*, 107–14, 121–25

Elephant Rock, skirmish at, 48, 53
Ellis County Historical Museum, 61–62
Evans, C. D., home of, 149

Far West steamer, *117*, 120
festivals, Buffalo Bill, 203–4
Fetterman Massacre Monument, *122*, 123
First Territorial Capitol State Historic Site, 12, *12*
Forrest, Nathan Bedford, 40
Fort Buford, officers' row at, *120*
Fort Buford State Historic Site, 125
Fort Buford State Historic Site, Brotherton Quarters, *124*
Fort Caspar Museum and Historic Site, *35*, 35–36
Fort Cody Trading Post, 143, *143*
Fort D. A. Russell, 101, 107
 post headquarters of, *110*
Fort Dodge, 52
Fort Fetterman, *117*
Fort Fetterman State Historic Site, 121–22
 visitor center, *121*
Fort Fred Steele State Historic Site, 83–84
Fort Harker Museum, 49
 guardhouse, *50*
Fort Hays
 Fifth Infantry Band before officers' quarters at, *47*
 site of first, 49
Fort Hays State Historic Site, 61
 restored officers' quarters at, *61*
Fort Kearny, Nebraska, *16*
Fort Kearny State Historical Park, 25–26
 army wagons and blacksmith shop at, *26*
Fort Laramie National Historic Site, 107–11, *110*
Fort Larned, *46*

Fort Larned National Historic Site,
  50–52
  restored buildings of, *52*
Fort Leavenworth, 23
Fort Lyon, 53
  Kit Carson Memorial Chapel at, *53*
Fort McPherson, 64–68, *65*
  recommended reading, 69
  sites, 68–69
  sole remaining structure from, *69*
Fort McPherson National Cemetery,
  68, 68–69
Fort McPherson Trail, sandstone
  marker, 84, *84*
Fort Phil Kearny State Historic Site,
  122–23
Fort Reno, *81*, 85–86
  parade grounds, *85*
Fort Robinson, 113
Fort Robinson State Park, *112*
Fort Sidney Complex, 129
  officers' quarters, *130*
Fort Sill, 86
Fort Supply
  guardhouse, *85*
  historic site, 84
Fort Wallace, *48*
Fort Wallace Cemetery, 52
Fort Wallace Memorial Museum, 52
Fort Yates, 167, *168*, 169–70
  guardhouse, *170*
Fort Zarah, 49–50
Fourth of July celebration, 8–9, 134–35
Free-Staters, 9–10, 13
Frontier Army Museum, 23

Garland, John Watts, Sir, 79
Garlow, Fred, death of, 202
Garlow, William, 202
Garnier, Baptistie "Little Bat,"
  gravesite, *68*
Ghost Dance movement, 167
Glur, Louis, 149
Glur's Tavern, 148–49, *149*

Godfrey, Edward S., 116
Golden Rule House, 42, 44
Goodman, Ed, 179
Goodman, Julia and Al, 136
Gore, George, Sir, 79
Grasshopper Falls, 9
Great Sioux War, 104
Green, Elisha, *150*
Grey, Zane, 194
Grierson, Benjamin H., 40
Grouard, Frank, 116

Hat Creek Station, *103*, 111, *111*
Hays City, Kansas, 56–57
Hazen, William B., 46
Hickok, James Butler "Wild Bill,"
  16, *17–19*, 39, 41, 44, 97
Hollenberg, Gerat H., 33
Hollenberg Pony Express Station
  State Historic Site, 32–33
A Hunting Expedition on the Plains
  (Alexandrovich), 90

Ice, Gary, 196
Independence Rock, 36
Irma Hotel, 180, *180*, 183, 184, *184*

John Brown Museum State Historic
  Site, 13
Judson, Edward Z. C., *see* Buntline,
  Ned
Jules, Rene, 28

Kanopolis, Kansas, 49
Kansas, first territorial capital of, 24
Kansas Pacific, Indian raid on, 44–45
King, Charles, 72, 101
Kit Carson Memorial Chapel at Fort
  Lyon, *53*

Leavenworth, Kansas, *8*
  sites, 10, 21–23, *22*
Leavenworth Daily Conservative, 57
Leavenworth Landing, 21

Leavenworth Landing Park, 23
LeClaire, Iowa, sites, *3*, 4–6
Lillie, Gordon, 164
Lincoln County Courthouse, 140
Lincoln County Historical Museum, 69
   Fort McPherson structure at, *69*
Little Bighorn, news from, 102
The Lives and Legends of Buffalo Bill
   (Russell), 10
Lookout Mount, Cody gravesite at,
   198–99
Loup River, South Fork of the, *66–67*

McLaughlin, James, 167–69
Madsen, Christian, 103
Majors, Alexander, 155
The Making of Buffalo Bill (Walsh), 18
maps
   Cody, Wyoming sites, *185*
   Cody sites, *xii*
   1876 Sioux Campaign sites, *106*
   Leavenworth, Kansas sites, *22*
   LeClaire, Iowa sites, *3*
   North Platte, Nebraska sites, *139*
   Southern Plains sites, *51*
Marais des Cynges Massacre State
   Historic site, 13
Marmaduke, John S., 40
Marsh, Grant, 120
Mather, Stephen, 183
Mathewson, William E. "Buffalo
   Bill," *58*
Medals of Honor, *66–67*
Merritt, Wesley, *101*, 101–2
Miles, Nelson A., 81–83, 117,
   167–69, 173
   and Cody viewing Indian camp, *172*
"Millionaires Hunt," 80–81
Mills, Anson, 65, 101
Milner, Moses "California Joe," 65
   gravesite, *68*
Missouri-Yellowstone Confluence
   Interpretive Center, 125
Moran, Breck, gravesite, 190

Morlacchi, Giuseppina, 96, *96*
Mount Aurora Cemetery, view of,
   from Pilot Knob, *11*
Mount Hope Cemetery, 98–99
Mount Moriah Cemetery, *19*
My Life on the Plains (Custer), 44,
   90, *109*

National Historic Trails Interpretive
   Center, *35*
National Pony Express Association,
   Pony Express Trail event, 37
Nebraska, winter hunting expedition
   in, 20–21
Nebraska Hall of Fame, 203
   Cody bust in, *203*
New York Herald, 90
Ninth Kansas Volunteers, 39
North, Frank, 64, *73*, 145
   Cody partnership, 127–28
   Columbus home, 148, *148*
   death of, *74*, 146
   gravesite, 147–48, *148*
   military services for, 146
   and the Pawnee Scouts, *73–75*
   state historical marker, 148
North, James, 145
North, Luther, 29, 64, *73–74*
   gravesite, 147–48
   state historical marker, 148
   on Tall Bull death, 74
North Platte, Nebraska
   Codys' move to, 134–38
   Fourth of July celebration, 134–35
   recommended reading, 143
   related attractions, 143
   sites, 138–43, *139*
North Platte Station, Post at, 133
   officers' quarters, 138
   surgeon's quarters, *138*

Oakley, Annie, 142, 159, *160*
Old Freighters Museum, *24*, 25
Old Glory Blow-Out, 134–35

Olinger's Mortuary, 198
Omaha, Nebraska, 151–55
    sites, 156
Omaha Driving Park, 156
Omohundro, Texas Jack, *18*, 96,
    96, 120, *150*
101 Ranch Wild West Show,
    164–65, *165*
Oregon and Santa Fe Trails, 23
Original Parade Ground, 24
Osawatomie, Battle of, 13
Outdoor Life magazine, 193
Overton, Eugene, *150*

Pahaska Tepee, 183, 191, *191*
Patee House Museum, 31
Pawnee Scouts, *73–75*
    photograph of, *75*
    recommended reading, *75*
Paxton Hotel, *153*, 156
Pine Ridge Reservation, Cody and
    Burke at, *174*
Platte Bridge Station, *35*
Poker Church, 187, *188*
Pollock, Oliver C. C., 120
Pony Express, 28–30
    recommended reading, 37
    related events, 37
    route, Buffalo Bill's historic, 36–37
    sites, 30–37
    stations, *32*, 33
    statue of horse and rider, 30–31
Pony Express Barn, 32
Pony Express National Museum,
    31, 31–32
Post Sutler's Home, 23, *23*
Potato Creek Johnny, *19*
Pourier, Baptiste "Big Bat," 116
Prairie Dog Creek, 20

Red Cloud, gravesite, 177, *177*
Red Cloud Agency, 113–14
Red Legged Scouts, 39
Republican River campaign, 64

Riverside Cemetery, 188
Rock Creek Station State Historical
    Park, 33
rodeos, one of first, 134–35
Rome, Kansas, 56–57
    obelisk marking site of, *60*
The Rookery, 24
Roosevelt, Theodore, 179–80
Rose, William, 56
Rosebud, 116–17
Rosebud Battlefield State Park, 124
Royal Buffalo Hunt of 1872, *87*,
    88–92, *89*
    commemorative marker, *92*
    recommended reading, 93
    sites, 93
Russell, Don, 10, 107, 145
Russell, William, 28
Russell, Majors and Waddell, 28
    Cody working for, 15–20
    headquarters of, 21

Sage Creek, camp at, 111
Saline River, battle of, 44–45, *45*
Salsbury, Nate, 158, *162*
    death of, 163
Salt Creek Valley, 8
    view of, from Government Hill, *7*
Sandoz, Mari, 105
Scotts Bluff National Monument,
    34–35
Scouts of the Prairie (play), 96–97
    advertisement for, *97*
    stars of, *96*
Scout's Rest Ranch, *135*, 136
    barn, *142*, 142–43
    French Second Empire home at,
        141, 141–43
    public notice identifying, *136*
    traveling desk at, 141
Seventh Kansas Volunteer
    Cavalry, 40
Sheridan, Philip, 46–47, *47*, 54, 79,
    88, *89*

Sheridan Inn, *123*, 123–24
Sherman, William Tecumseh,
    21–23, 41
Sherman, Ewing and McCook,
    law offices of, 21–23
Simpson, Lewis, 16
Sitting Bull, 159
    arrest and death of, 167–69
    with Buffalo Bill cabinet card, *166*
    cabin on the Grand River, 171
    gravesite, 170, *171*
    recommended reading, 171
    sites, 169–71
Slade, Jack, 28
Slaughter, William J., 173
Slim Buttes, battle of, *118*
Southern Plains campaign
    Cody as scout during, 44–49
    first victory for U.S. Army in, 54
    sites, 49–54, *51*
Split Rock Station, 37
    site of, *36*
Spring Creek, Cody wounded at, 48
Stagecoach Museum, 111–13
stained glass, Cody family, 140, *140*
State of Nebraska steamship, 160, *161*
    passenger list, *161*
Steinhauer, Fred, 202
Stilwell, Jack, 83
Summit Springs, Battle of, 64, 71–76
    Cheyenne herd boy memorial at
        site of, *76*
    recommended reading, 77
    rescue, *70*
    sites, 76–77
Syracuse Houses, 24

Tall Bull, *71*
    death of, 72–76
Tammen, Harry, 164
Tarr, Ebb, gravesite, 190
Taylor, Buck, 159
TE Ranch, 179–83, 189
    house at, *179*

Terry, Alfred, 116–117, 120
Thomas, Chauncey, Cody interview by,
    193–94
Three Crossings Station, *27*
Trails of Yesterday (Bratt), 128
Trans-Mississippi Exposition, 155
    advertisement for Cody Day at, *155*
    Grand Court of, *154*
Triplett, Frank, 45
True West magazine, 200
Tupelo, Battle of, 40

U. S. Indian Police, gravesite, 170–171
Union Depot, 21
Ups and Downs of an Army Officer
    (Armes), *45*

Victoria, Queen of England, 161

Walsh, Richard J., 18
Warbonnet
    battlefield, *112*
    monument overlooking battlefield
        at, *113*
    recommended reading, 114
    sites, 107–14
    skirmish at, 102–7
Warbonnet Historic Site, 114
Ward, Henry, gravesite, 99
Warren ICBM and Heritage
    Museum, 107
Washita Battlefield National Historic
    Site, 54
Webb, William, 56–57
Weichell, Maria, 71
Welcome Wigwam home
    first, 134, 138–40
    second, 136–37, *137*, 140
Weston, Missouri, 10–12
Wetmore, Helen Cody, 105
Whistler, Joseph, 121
Wichita Mountains National Wildlife
    Refuge, 86
    buffalo, *86*

Wild West, 145–47
  advertisement for, *152*
  in Omaha, Nebraska, 151–53
  see also Buffalo Bill's Wild West
Wilde, Oscar, 161
World's Columbian Exposition, 161
Wounded Knee, 173–74
  massacre site, 174–77
  memorial to those slain at, *176*
  recommended reading, 177

Wyndham-Quin, Windham Thomas,
  Earl of Dunraven, *79*, 79–80

Yellow Hair
  death of, 104–7
  monument marking site of where
    Cody killed, *105*

Zietz, Henry, 200

Other Titles
by Jeff Barnes

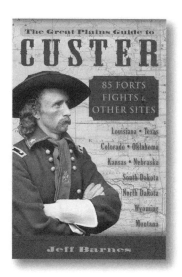
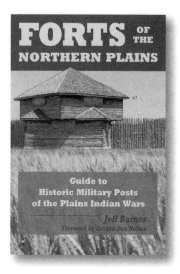

The Great Plains Guide to Custer:
85 Forts, Fights, & Other Sites
9780811708364

Forts of the Northern Plains:
Guide to Historic Military Posts
of the Plains Indian Wars
9780811734967